THE SAMURAI

STEPHEN TURNBULL

OSPREY
PUBLISHING

First published in Great Britain in 2016 by Osprey Publishing,
PO Box 883, Oxford, OX1 9PL, UK
1385 Broadway, 5th Floor, New York, NY 10018, USA
E-mail: info@ospreypublishing.com

Osprey Publishing, part of Bloomsbury Publishing Plc

This volume comprises text previously published in the following books
by Stephen Turnbull: *Samurai: The World of the Warrior*; *Warriors
of Medieval Japan*; *The Samurai and the Sacred* and Weapon 29 *Katana:
The Samurai Sword*. With supplementary material from the following
books by Anthony J. Bryant: Elite 23 *The Samurai*; Warrior 7 *Samurai
1550–1600*. Artwork by Angus McBride and Peter Dennis, previously
published in Warrior 7 and *Strongholds of the Samurai*, respectively.

A CIP catalogue record for this book is available from the British Library.

Stephen Turnbull has asserted his right under the Copyright, Designs
and Patents Act, 1988, to be identified as the Author of this Work.

ISBN: 9781472813725
PDF ISBN: 9781472813732
ePub ISBN: 9781472813749
Typeset in Garamond and Helvetica Neue
Originated by PDQ Digital Media Solutions
Printed in China through World Print Ltd

16 17 18 19 20 10 9 8 7 6 5 4 3 2 1

www.ospreypublishing.com

DEDICATION

This book is dedicated to Sue Brayshaw and John Head who got married
on 2 April 2016, with best wishes.

IMAGE ACKNOWLEDGEMENTS

All images are from the Author's collection unless otherwise specified.

Opposite: Minamoto Yoshiie leads his samurai into action during the
so-called 'Later Three Years War'. (Stephen Turnbull/Japan Archive)

Contents page: Samurai in mounted combat. Detail of painted screen
scenes from the 12th-century Gempei War, Tosa School, Edo Period,
early 17th century. (Photo by DeAgostini/Getty Images)

Cover: Menju Ietora, the standard-bearer of Shibata Katsuie, fights to
defend his golden Shinto *gohei* standard from the enemy.

A NOTE ON DATES

For the convenience of readers the lunar dates used in the primary
sources have been converted to the Western calendar.

A NOTE ON NAMES

Following conventional Japanese usage, all names are given with the
surname first (e.g. Minamoto Yoritomo). Those mentioned in the text
are referred to by their given name after the first mention (e.g. Minamoto
Yoritomo, thereafter referred to as Yoritomo). In the final chapter,
the surname is used.

JAPANESE WORDS

A glossary of the key Japanese words and phrases that appear in the text
can be found at the end of this work. These words appear in italics at
their first mention.

Osprey Publishing supports the Woodland Trust, the UK's leading
woodland conservation charity. Between 2014 and 2018 our donations
will be spent on their Centenary Woods project in the UK.

CONTENTS

INTRODUCTION

The samurai were the legendary warriors of old Japan who led noble and violent lives governed by the demands of honour, personal integrity and loyalty. They are defined in the modern imagination by the deadly swords that they carried and their famous code: *bushido*, the way of the warrior. But their martial prowess was just one facet of the lives of these iconic fighters. This book goes beyond the battlefield to explore all aspects of samurai life, throwing light on their home lives, religious and social background as well as cultural accomplishments. It provides a romp through samurai history, from the origins of the warrior class to its abolition in the 19th century. In other words, it presents a brief history of the samurai from swords to suits, from top-knots to top hats.

ANCESTORS OF THE SAMURAI

Ancient Japan was dominated by several rival clans, but by AD 400 one had emerged triumphant in the struggle. The name by which the victors are known to history is Yamato, and they are key figures because the Yamato rulers are the ancestors of the Japanese imperial line.

LEFT In spite of all the emphasis in *Heike Monogatari (The Tale of the Heike)* on individual heroics and single combat, many of the battles of the Gempei War were won by setting fire to a building and then attacking the defenders as they ran out.

We know very little about the historical processes that took place to give power to the Yamato state, although many pointers have been gleaned from archaeology. Instead the origins of the imperial line are contained in some very colourful legends written down as a series of creation myths when the emperor system had become well established. They are preserved as the *Kojiki* (*The Record of Ancient Events*) of AD 712 and the *Nihongi* (*The Chronicles of Japan*) of AD 720. These legends of gods and heroes tell us nothing of wars between tribesmen or of one clan dominating the others. Such activities have to be inferred from tales of gods slaying serpents in distant lands. The best-known myth, and the one that is fundamental to understanding the cult of the emperor which retained its power through the ages even to the 20th century, tells how Amaterasu the sun goddess founded the Japanese imperial line when she sent her grandson down from heaven to rule the 'land of luxuriant rice fields'.

Many challenges were made by rival *uji* (the ancient clans) against the dominance assumed by the Yamato rulers. All were ultimately unsuccessful and, by the 7th century, the imperial line felt sufficiently secure to introduce far-reaching legislative changes for Japan. The Taika reforms of 646 were an ambitious set of edicts that sought to curtail any remaining power possessed by the surviving clans by making all of Japan subject to the emperor. One of the first tasks of the reforms was to establish Japan's first permanent capital city. This was achieved after a couple of false starts at Nara in 710. Buddhism, introduced to Japan two centuries earlier, flourished in the settled conditions of Nara. The government of Japan, like the design of the capital itself, was modelled on Tang China, and for some time the combination of the two provided a stable society.

Any dissatisfied clans, any individuals rebelling against the throne, or trouble from the recently pacified *emishi* (the tribesmen who had been pushed to the north

ABOVE This painted scroll depicts a samurai the Gosannen War of the 11th century. Note the bearskin boots and the wooden reel used for carrying a spare bowstring.

over the centuries) were dealt with efficiently. Kyoto succeeded Nara as the imperial capital of Japan in 894, a position it was to keep until 1868.

THE FIRST SAMURAI

The 10th century is the time that we first see the term 'samurai', literally 'those who serve', being used in a purely military context. At first it referred to men who went up to the imperial capital, Kyoto, to provide guard duty. In time it began to denote a military man who served any powerful landlord. The word rapidly acquired a strong aristocratic and hereditary aspect, so that samurai lineages began to be recognised and valued. Some were the descendants of the ancient clans of Japan. Others were newly established families whose reputations were secured by military prowess and whose glorious pedigrees were just starting to be written.

The service that the samurai families rendered to the Heian (Kyoto) court made them even more wealthy and powerful, and by the 11th century two particularly strong clans had emerged. They were the Taira and the Minamoto, and their exploits were to dominate Japanese politics for the next 100 years. Samurai from the two families took part on both sides during the Hogen Rebellion of 1156, an armed encounter in Kyoto that was concerned with the imperial succession. It was not long before another succession dispute put the Taira and the Minamoto into

LEFT The abduction of the former Emperor Go-Shirakawa by Fujiwara No Nobuyori during the Heiji Rebellion in 1159. Go-Shirakawa was later freed and Nobuyori killed, by Taira no Kiyomori, who founded Japan's first samurai-dominated government. Chromolithograph after an illustration by the monk Keion in *Heiji Monogatari* (*Tales of the Year Heiji*), 13th century. (Photo by Ann Ronan Pictures/ Print Collector/Getty Images)

direct opposition. The Taira were victorious in the struggle (the Heiji Rebellion of 1159–1160) and disposed ruthlessly of their rivals. But in 1180 the survivors of the Minamoto purge, key members of whom had been children spared by the Taira, reopened hostilities at the first battle of Uji. This was the first armed conflict in a war that was to become known as the Gempei War, from the Chinese reading of their names: 'Gen' for the Minamoto (Genji) and 'Hei' for the Taira (Heike).

The Gempei War is fundamental to understanding samurai history. First, the battles that took place such as Ichinotani (1184), Yashima (1185) and Dannoura (1185) created benchmarks for samurai excellence that were to last for the whole of samurai history. Heroic tales and works of art logged the incidents in the Gempei War as a verbal and visual catalogue of heroism that would show future generations the most noble, brave and correct ways of being a samurai. Nearly all the factors that were to become indelible parts of samurai culture have a reference point somewhere within the Gempei War. Prowess at archery and hand-to-hand fighting, the juxtaposition of art, poetry and violence, undying loyalty to one's lord and the tremendous tradition of ritual suicide all feature in the tales of the Gempei War.

The other way in which the Gempei War made its mark on samurai history lay in the steps the victors took to confirm their triumph. In 1192 Minamoto Yoritomo took the title of *shogun*. This was the rank that had previously been bestowed temporarily on samurai leaders who had accepted an imperial commission to deal with rebels against the throne. Yoritomo, whose family was now unchallenged in Japan, took the title for himself for his new role as military dictator. The difference was that the temporary imperial commission had now become a permanent one and was not relinquished until another eight centuries had passed and Japan had entered the modern age in 1868. The position of shogun was also made hereditary within the Minamoto family.

ABOVE The Heian Shrine in Kyoto was built in 1895 as a partial reproduction of the Heian Imperial Palace. (Photo by Alvin Leong/Flickr)

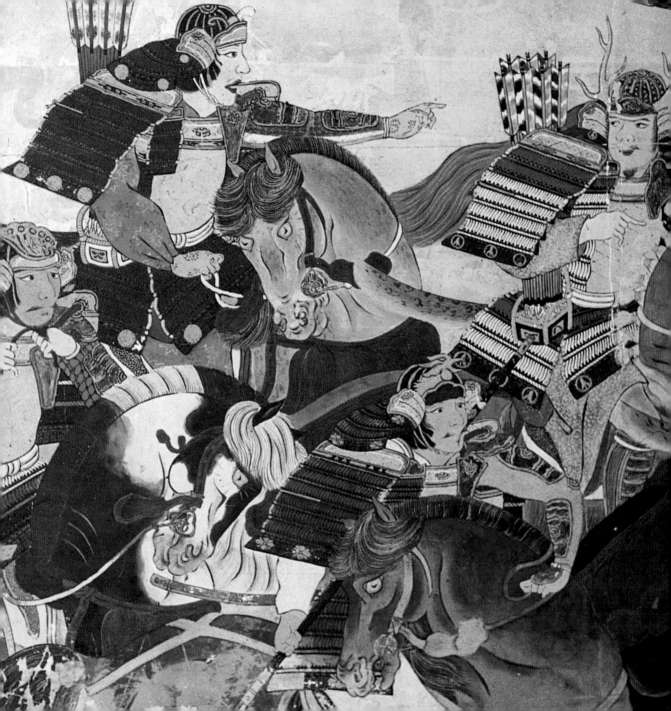

Government exercised by the shogun was called the *bakufu*, a name derived from the *maku*, the curtains that surrounded a general's headquarters on a battlefield. It was a good choice for a new system of ruling that relegated the emperor to the position of figurehead with immense religious – but no political – power. The control of Japan's affairs now lay with the leader of the greatest family of samurai.

CHALLENGES TO THE SAMURAI

The Minamoto did not have long to enjoy their success. Yoritomo was killed in a riding accident in 1199, and their dynasty only lasted two more generations before they were overthrown by the Hojo. Out of respect for the tradition of the title staying with the Minamoto, the Hojo rulers styled themselves regents rather than shoguns. It was therefore the Hojo *shikken* (regency), not the Minamoto bakufu, that faced a brief attempt at imperial restoration in 1221. This was speedily dealt with, and another half century was to pass before the Hojo took the brunt of a very different threat to the survival of Japan itself.

The 13th century in continental Asia was the time of the Mongols. Under the leadership of Genghis Khan and his successors these fierce horsemen had broken out from their steppe homelands and gone on to conquer distant lands, from Korea to Poland. Japan entered their sights in 1274, when the Mongols raided the southern island of Kyushu. This was followed by a serious attempt at invasion in 1281 that was driven off by a combination of samurai bravery and a knockout blow delivered by

LEFT The samurai was essentially a mounted warrior. In this painted screen of the battle of Yashima in 1185 we see samurai of the Minamoto clan. In the foreground, two samurai, one of whom is on foot, wield *naginata*, the Japanese glaives with long curved blades.

THE IMPERIAL REGALIA

While many nations publicly display their regalia of sovereignty, there is one notable exception: no visit to Japan will ever include a trip to see the Japanese crown jewels. Not even the emperor of Japan has seen any item of his own regalia since the 12th century.

The three items – the mirror, the sword and the jewel – were, and still are, the legitimators of kingship: the symbols and guarantees of the eternity of the imperial throne. Their origins are bound up in legends of the creation of the imperial dynasty itself. The story goes that when the sun goddess Amaterasu hid in a cave, the other *kami* (spirits) tempted her out with a story about a rival, more powerful kami and the sound of music and revelry. When she looked out, she saw a jewel hanging on a tree and next to it the face of her new rival. Before she had time to realise that it was her own reflection in a bronze mirror, the other kami seized her and prevented her from retreating to the cave.

The third item appears later in a myth which tells how the kami Susano-o destroyed a fierce serpent with eight heads and tails, and discovered a sword hidden in its tail section. As it was a very fine sword, he presented it to his sister Amaterasu, and because the serpent's tail had been covered in black clouds the sword was named *Ame no murakumo no tsurugi*, the Cloud-Cluster Sword. (It later became known as *Kusanagi no tsurugi*, the Grass-Mowing Sword, after it was used by Prince Yamato to cut his way through burning grass to escape an attempt on his life.)

Amaterasu handed the sacred sword, the mirror and the jewel to her grandson Ninigi, who in turn passed them on to his grandson Jimmu (traditionally 660–585 BC), identified as the first emperor of Japan. The regalia were then handed down in the imperial line, becoming a vital possession for any candidate for the succession.

In early samurai history, however, the regalia that rival imperial candidates vied with each other to possess were not the actual crown jewels, but the officially recognised replicas. Those of the mirror and sword were created by Emperor Sujin in the 1st century BC. They were accorded the same reverence as the originals, while the originals were transferred to the Grand Shrine of Ise.

Over subsequent centuries the regalia featured dramatically in conflicts, notably the decisive sea battle of Dannoura between the Taira and Minamoto in 1185. Betrayed by their allies and realising that the battle was lost, many of the Taira committed suicide by jumping into the sea; among them was the emperor's

A detail from a painted screen of the battle of Dannoura in 1185 showing the two fleets engaging in battle. The red flags of the Taira family are flying from the vessel in the centre, which is under attack from the Minamoto.

grandmother with the child emperor, the replica sword and the sacred jewel in her arms. Although the original jewel was recovered, the replica sword was lost forever.

Emperor Meiji was enthroned in Kyoto in 1868. In the same year Japan's capital, along with the replica mirror and the original jewel, was moved to Tokyo (then called Edo), the city that had been the shogun's

capital since 1603. There, the two sacred objects are housed within the imperial palace. The original mirror is still in the Ise inner shrine, while the original Grass-Mowing Sword lies in the Atsuta Shrine in Nagoya. The sacred replica sword, of course, still lies at the bottom of the sea off Dannoura, if it has not yet completely rusted away.

ABOVE Minamoto Yoshitsune and the warrior monk Benkei (with naginata) at the battle of Yashima in 1185, from a painted screen in the Watanabe Museum, Tottori.

the weather. The fateful storm was the famous *kamikaze*, the 'wind of the gods' that destroyed the Mongol fleet as it lay at anchor. The repulse of the Mongols added a further set of reference points to sit alongside the experiences of the Gempei War in the world of the samurai. As late as 1945 the term kamikaze still had such a powerful resonance of the destruction of an invader that it was adopted as the name for the suicide pilots who crashed their planes into American ships.

The next major challenge posed to samurai hegemony during the 14th century came from a further attempt at imperial restoration. This movement, led by the energetic emperor Go-Daigo, was ultimately no more successful than the brief venture of 1221. But its execution was more prolonged, and succeeded in adding more names to the pantheon of samurai heroes and more glorious exploits to the litany of the Gempei War and the Mongol invasions. In particular, these Nanbokucho Wars or 'Wars Between the Courts' (so called because for a time there were two rival emperors) produced one samurai who was to be celebrated for centuries because of his loyalty to the person of the emperor. His name was Kusunoki Masashige. When the imperial line was finally restored during the 19th century, he was the exemplar from history who was presented to the loyalist samurai as the ideal they should follow. Sadly for Masashige, his devotion to the imperial cause led to his suicide at the battle of Minatogawa in 1336. The battle was fought against Masashige's advice, and the inevitable defeat that was the result of his obedience to the imperial will required the ultimate sacrifice. Go-Daigo's attempted coup had one other result, because when the Hojo regents were overthrown the power gap was filled by the Ashikaga family. As they were of Minamoto descent, they re-established the bakufu and ruled Japan as shoguns for the following 200 years. But once again a single ruling family found it impossible to keep under control the numerous volatile and powerful samurai families. The 15th century in Japan is therefore a catalogue of apparently minor clan squabbles settled by force, until one such dispute affected the heart of government itself. This was the tragic Onin War, fought from 1467 to 1476. When the fighting was over, Kyoto was in ruins, the shogun was disgraced and a number of civil wars were taking place elsewhere in Japan.

THE PERIOD OF WARRING STATES

The Onin War ushered in a century and a half of conflict to which historians have given the name *Sengoku Jidai*, the Period of Warring States, a term taken from the Chinese histories, although the Japanese wars were between clans and families rather than between states as such. Their leaders called themselves *daimyo*, which literally means 'great names', and 16th-century daimyo such as Takeda Shingen, Uesugi Kenshin and Date Masamune were to make 'great names' for themselves that eclipsed anything their heroic ancestors may have achieved during the Gempei War. It was also a time of great developments in samurai warfare. Only the strong survived, and to be strong involved fielding large armies armed with good weapons. The successful daimyo had ready access to large numbers of troops by using *ashigaru* (footsoldiers), whom they trained to use bows (once the traditional samurai weapon), long spears and the newly introduced firearms. Crude Chinese handguns had been known since 1510, but the introduction of European arquebuses in 1543 caused something of a military revolution. The European traders were the initial source of supply, but the Japanese soon turned their hands to manufacture and production. It took a little longer before the effective use of the weapons came to be realised when the celebrated daimyo Oda Nobunaga began to use volley-firing by trained infantry squads. His victory at the battle of Nagashino in 1575 drew heavily on these new techniques.

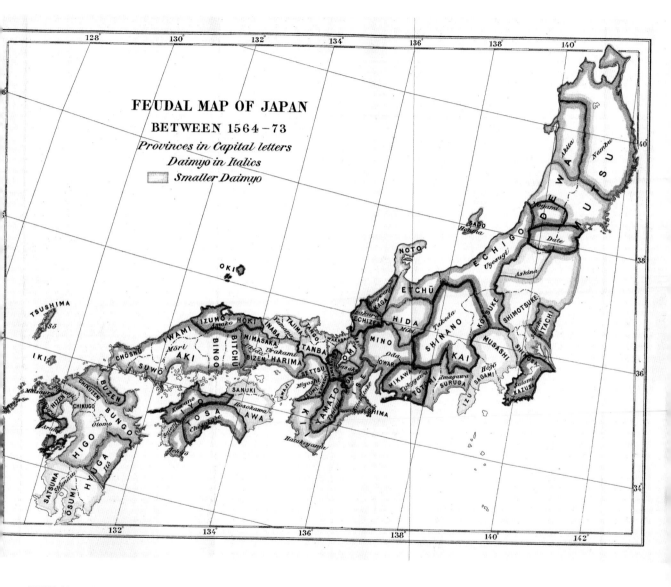

ABOVE Map of Japan showing the provinces and major daimyo in the period 1564–73. (James Murdoch and Isoh Yamagata/ Wikimedia Commons/CC-BY-SA 3.0)

INTRODUCTION

The major military contests in the Sengoku Jidai were the struggles for power between the most powerful daimyo, out of whose ranks there would ultimately be only one winner. Oda Nobunaga was the first daimyo to take steps in that direction when he occupied Kyoto and abolished the shogunate in 1568. He died in 1582. The eventual reunifier of Japan turned out to be one of Oda Nobunaga's samurai who had risen through the ranks from his initial position as an ashigaru. Toyotomi Hideyoshi had become one of Nobunaga's most trusted generals, and reacted with a mixture of loyalty and opportunism when he heard the news that Oda Nobunaga had been assassinated. In a series of political moves and military campaigns such as the battles of Yamazaki (1582) and Shizugatake (1583), Hideyoshi asserted his authority. Some daimyo became his allies after failing to beat him in battle. Tokugawa Ieyasu, who was defeated at the battle of Nagakute in 1584, is the best example of this accommodative approach. Others proved to be more stubborn, and in 1585, in his first campaign off Japan's main island of Honshu, Hideyoshi conquered the island of Shikoku. In 1587 he followed this up by the subjugation of Kyushu and the mighty Shimazu family, until, with the submission of the northern daimyo in 1591, Hideyoshi controlled the whole of Japan. His humble origins prevented him from re-establishing the shogunate, but his power was greater than the shogun's had ever been.

It was only then that Hideyoshi began to overreach himself with an attempted conquest of China. The invasion of Korea that he launched in 1592 was intended to be the first stage of the plan, but Ming China rose to the challenge and a fierce war began. The combination of the Chinese invasion, the Korean navy with its famous turtle ships

LEFT Nobunaga was the first of Japan's three unifiers. He conquered much of central Japan through his combination of military skill and utter ruthlessness. In this modern painting we see Nobunaga mounted on a horse wearing an elaborate suit of multi-coloured armour. An ashigaru groom leads the horse, while his flag bearer follows on behind.

and the activities of Korean guerrillas ensured that the Japanese expeditionary force never got further than the Korean peninsula. It was finally and ignominiously driven out in 1598, having achieved nothing other than the devastation of its nearest neighbour.

By the time of the Japanese evacuation from the mainland Hideyoshi was dead, and the nominal ruler of Japan was now his 5-year-old son Hideyori. It was a situation that could not last long in the hothouse of samurai politics. Soon two rival factions emerged: those who were loyal to Hideyori, and those who saw the future in the person of Tokugawa Ieyasu, the one daimyo who was powerful enough, and clever enough, to challenge the succession. The two sides met at Sekigahara in 1600, one of the most decisive battles in Japanese history. Ieyasu was victorious. As he was of Minamoto descent, he was able to become shogun, and Tokugawa shoguns ruled Japan until the mid-19th century. In 1614 there was a brief and very worrying attempt by Hideyori to claim back his inheritance, but this only led to the huge sieges of Osaka conducted in the winter of 1614 and the summer of 1615. Osaka was a total victory for the Tokugawa. The survivors of the sieges were liquidated, and apart from the short-lived Shimabara Rebellion of 1638 no other military challenge threatened Tokugawa primacy for two more centuries.

THE PASSING OF THE SAMURAI

The means by which the Tokugawa shoguns asserted their authority were many and varied. The shock provided by the Shimabara Rebellion, which had a fanatical Christian element to it, prompted the government to sever all its connections

RIGHT Toyotomi Hideyoshi, the second unifier of Japan.

with Europe. There had long been a suspicion that Catholic missionaries were acting as stalking horses for the European powers. They also provided the contacts through which a rebel against the Tokugawa could obtain European weapons. The bakufu's Exclusion Edict of 1639 banned all foreign trade except through carefully controlled outlets. China and Korea remained as trading partners, but the sole contact with Europe for the following 200 years was through a handful of Protestant Dutch merchants who were allowed to reside on the artificial island of Dejima in Nagasaki harbour.

To control any potential rivals at home, the daimyo were given responsibilities for ruling their own territories (the *han*) under the overall control of the Tokugawa. It was a system backed up by constant surveillance and by measures such as the Alternate Attendance System. The basis of this was nothing more than a colossal hostage system. The daimyo resided in their castle towns while their families lived in Edo, the shogun's capital. The daimyo would meet them when they made their annual visit to Edo to pay their respects to the shogun. They were required to march

ABOVE Tokugawa Ieyasu, from a hanging scroll in the Nagashino Castle Memorial Hall.

RIGHT Ii Naomasa made a glowing red the hallmark of his retainers. The colour appeared on their body armour, their helmets, their banners, their horses' harnesses and even on the minor parts of samurai armour such as the sleeves, so the Ii samurai are always the easiest to recognise on painted screens. This screen illustrates Ii Naomasa's involvement at the battle of Sekigahara in 1600, and is in the Watanabe Museum, Tottori.

there at the head of a huge army equipped with the finest armour and weapons – a clever ploy designed to keep them as busy and as poor as possible. This happy state of affairs continued until Western ships began appearing in Japanese waters in the early 19th century. The sightings culminated in the brief appearance of Commodore Matthew C. Perry's US fleet in 1853, followed by his formidable return in 1854. Trade concessions were demanded. Impressed and fearful of the power of the outside world, the Tokugawa government began to sign trading treaties and opened up their ports to foreigners. This aroused much anger among traditionalists in Japanese society, who felt that the shogun was abandoning key Japanese values and allowing himself to be disadvantaged through fear of the 'Western barbarians'.

The main opposition to the shogun's policy of opening up Japan came from daimyo such as the Mori of Choshu and the Shimazu of Satsuma, whose ancestors had suffered under the Tokugawa. These critics were equally awed by the military might of the West, but sought to learn new military techniques so that Japan could be defended. Soon two separate aims developed among the traditionalists: the overthrow of the shogunate, and the expulsion of foreigners. Both these intentions came together in the symbolic figure of the emperor. To the slogan of 'Sonno joi' ('Honour the emperor and expel the barbarians'), the opponents of the Tokugawa sought to replace the shogun by force and to restore power to the emperor. A civil war followed that was fought with great bitterness and devotion on both sides. There had been two failed attempts at imperial restoration in the past, but this third attempt, known as the Meiji Restoration, fully succeeded. A few diehards, such as the loyal samurai of Aizu in northern Japan, fought for the shogun until they were completely crushed by the forces of modernity. In 1868 the last Tokugawa shogun handed back to the new emperor the imperial commission to rule that had been granted to Minamoto Yoritomo in 1192.

ABOVE This Japanese print shows (left to right) Captain Henry Adams, Commodore Matthew C. Perry, and a Commander Anan. (Library of Congress, Washington)

Emperor Meiji was restored to a level of political power that the occupant of the role had not enjoyed for centuries, but the outcome of the 1868 Meiji Restoration was not the expulsion of the foreigners that its supporters had originally wanted. Instead there was an enthusiastic embracing of Western culture. It was a massive U-turn that most people saw as inevitable. There was also no room for a hereditary warrior class in the new Japan, so a European-style army replaced the sword-wearing samurai.

Many of the 'old guard' resented the changes, and there were some flickers of resistance, such as the Satsuma Rebellion of 1877. But apart from such doomed anachronisms Japan stepped squarely onto the modern stage, and the world of the samurai was left behind as a memory that would inspire the nation, terrify its enemies and mystify its allies for many years to come.

CHRONOLOGY

710	Nara established as imperial capital – start of Nara Period.
894	Kyoto succeeds Nara as imperial capital – start of Heian Period.
1156	Hogen Rebellion: a dispute over the imperial succession, which sows the seeds of the Gempei War.
1160	Heiji Rebellion: a succession dispute, which puts the Minamoto and Taira clans in direct opposition.
1180–85	Gempei War. After the defeat of the Taira at Dannoura, Minamoto Yoritomo assumes control and Kamakura Period begins.
1192	Minamoto Yoritomo becomes the first shogun.
1199–1256	Hojo shikken (regency).
1221	Attempt at imperial restoration by cloistered emperor Go-Toba is defeated.
1274	First Mongol attack on Kyushu fails.
1281	Second Mongol attack is defeated by the kamikaze.
1324	Ex-emperor Go-Daigo fails to overthrow the shogunate.
1336	Battle of Minatogawa. Takauji Masashige proclaims new emperor, and becomes first Ashikaga shogun, beginning the Muromachi Period. Go-Daigo forms his own imperial court at Yoshino. Beginning of Nanbokucho Wars (the Wars Between the Courts).

ABOVE The priest Mongaku goads Minamoto Yoritomo into rebellion by showing him the skull of his father, Minamoto Yoshitomo, who was murdered by the Taira.

1467–77	The Onin War, arising from a dispute between daimyo and involving the Ashikaga shogunate. Kyoto is devastated and the widespread conflict leads into the Sengoku Jidai.
1488	Militant Buddhist *Ikko-ikki* (mobs) take over the province of Kaga. Domination lasts until the 1570s.
1543	Arrival of Europeans and the introduction of arquebuses.
1549	Arquebuses used for the first time in Japanese warfare at Kajiki.
1568	Oda Nobunaga installs Ashikaga Yoshiaki as puppet shogun; beginning of Azuchi-Momoyama Period.
1573	Oda Nobunaga purges Ashikaga Yoshiaki and establishes his own government.
1574	The Ikko-ikki fortress of Nagashima is destroyed.
1575	Battle of Nagashino.
1576	Building of Azuchi Castle. Nobunaga attacks Ishiyama Honganji.
1580	Surrender of Ishiyama Honganji to Oda Nobunaga.
1582	Oda Nobunaga is assassinated; Toyotomi Hideyoshi takes up the goal of unification.
1588	Toyotomi Hideyoshi's Sword Hunt disarms all except the samurai class.
1591	Toyotomi Hideyoshi's unification of Japan completed. Separation Edicts divide samurai from farmers.
1592–98	Toyotomi Hideyoshi's invasion of Korea.
1598	Death of Toyotomi Hideyoshi.
1600	Battle of Sekigahara; the victor, Tokugawa Ieyasu, controls virtually all of Japan.

1603	Tokugawa Ieyasu becomes shogun; Edo Period begins.
1614 & 1615	Sieges of Osaka.
1633–39	Policies enacted which begin period of national isolation.
1702	Revenge carried out by the 47 *Ronin* (masterless samurai).
1638	Shimabara Rebellion.
1853	Japan's isolation is ended by the arrival of US warships in Edo Bay, bringing demands for a treaty.
1868	Meiji Restoration: imperial rule is restored.
1877	Satsuma Rebellion; siege of Kumamoto.

ABOVE Print by Yoshitoshi showing the defeated Satsuma rebels, 1877. (Photo by Universal History Archive/UIG via Getty Images)

THE WARRIOR LIFESTYLE

Samurai status was a matter of caste rather than occupation. All samurai, whether male or female, were part of the military class, regardless of whether they had ever picked up a sword. Samurai were not confined to a purely military role, however. Some samurai became scholars of great renown. They were civil and military administrators, clergymen, artists and aesthetes. Others were just family members. Yet all were expected to be familiar with their martial role.

Women were all trained in how to use the small dirks they carried in their *obi*, or waist sashes. Usually kept wrapped in a brocade case, this was as much a sign of their position as the sword was for the men. Upper-class women were also trained to use certain weapons: the naginata (a type of halberd) became a woman's weapon, used for the last-ditch defence of the home. Feudal lords had bands of naginata-armed women roaming the inner compounds of their castles at night.

Many members of the Buddhist clergy – at least most of rank – had been born into the samurai class. Although religion was one area where one's rank in life was

LEFT In this print we see the great samurai Uesugi Kenshin in the role of a connoisseur of swords. He is examining the detail of the workmanship on the blade by the reflected light of a fire. Note his shaven head – the mark of a samurai who was also a monk.

not supposed to matter (after all, one was supposed to have abandoned the ways of the world upon taking the tonsure), this was seldom the case. Some wealthy and very powerful lords took Buddhist vows, yet continued to govern their domains and lead vast armies: the daimyo Takeda Shingen (1521–73) and Uesugi Kenshin (1530–78) are two famous examples. For most ashigaru, the realities of life in the ranks ensured that dreams of glory remained just that. Ironically, it was Toyotomi Hideyoshi himself – the man who had risen from peasant-born sandal-bearer to the ruler of all Japan – who had made that dream even harder to achieve when he issued edicts restricting samurai status to those who had been so born.

The Confucian ethic of rigid social structures did not gain official recognition until the Tokugawa government – anxious to secure firm control over society – formally encouraged it. Nevertheless, there was a strong Confucian undercurrent, a sense of everyone accepting his or her lot. Conveniently, this was also a fatalistic Buddhist world view.

There was a great fear of losing one's master, and the social structure supported the inter-reliance of vassal and lord. To become lordless – a ronin (literally 'wave person') – meant the warrior was left without the support or protection of his clan. If the lord died and there was no heir, his retainers would all become ronin. A retainer could also be banished from the clan for a crime, such as brawling or violating regulations.

Ronin were wandering swords for hire, and often turned to banditry. Some maintained their sense of honour, and either took the tonsure, or found new employment

RIGHT In this unusual but informative painted scroll we see a group of senior samurai relaxing. One is having a massage, while *sake* (rice wine) is being served to his companions.

ABOVE The game of *go* had obvious connections to strategic planning. It is played on a heavy wooden board using black and white stones, kept here in wooden bowls. The samurai in the centre is wearing the standard *kamishimo*, which consists of *hakama* and a *kataginu*, the sleeveless jacket with projecting shoulders. On his head is an *eboshi*, a stiffened cap. The samurai on the left is wearing a kamishimo of a more relaxed day-to-day variety. The standing samurai is wearing the 'shorts' known as *han-bakama*. (Angus McBride © Osprey Publishing)

with another lord and gave allegiance to a new clan. During the Sengoku Jidai, there was no shortage of opportunities for lordless ex-samurai to redeem themselves.

All samurai had duties and were paid stipends, and from this they had to buy whatever of their equipment was not issued and furnish their household (if they had one). The basis for the economy was rice, and a unit of rice that could feed a man for a year – called a *koku* – was the universal measure of wealth. Fiefs and estates were described in the terms of how many koku of rice they produced. One koku is 120 litres. The lowest samurai received a little less than a koku (assuming his meals were all on the books of his lord's estate).

A middling lord, or castle commander, might receive a stipend of several hundred koku, and with that he had to pay the samurai in his service, supply his garrison, feed his horses, pay his servants, and so on. For convenience's sake, hard cash was used to make payments, but ultimately it was a rice-based economy. Even the Takeda of Kai, who sat on the most valuable gold mines in the nation, needed rice to feed their soldiers. Such was the importance of rice that many farmers did not get to eat the crop they grew for the samurai: they ate millet. The rice went to the lord's castles for measuring, then storage or dispersal.

The finances were left to the wives, as the samurai men deemed handling money beneath them. The only men who dealt with cash were those whose specific duties required it (overseer of the castle kitchens, for example). Even then, it would be notes exchanging hands, for later payment.

Various duties within the clan were assigned as official positions. In some ways, it was similar to a modern army: while everyone is a soldier, some are also cooks, some are clerks, some deal with transportation and some are responsible for other, more esoteric, duties.

Samurai in a garrison would be freely transferred from one position to the next if their work was good enough. Promotions were not always in the same area. In this way, if a warrior achieved a sufficiently high rank, he would be fairly conversant with all the details necessary to run and maintain an army, a garrison or even an entire domain.

EARLY YEARS

From *Hagakure* (*Hidden behind Leaves*), a collection of anecdotes and moral tales compiled by a certain Yamamoto Tsunetomo in about 1710, we read that a samurai should rise at four in the morning, bathe and arrange his hair daily, eat when the sun comes up and retire when it becomes dark. Within this tidy framework the samurai of the Sengoku Jidai led a full and busy life from a very early age. *Hagakure* even has advice for the parents of young samurai:

> There is a way of bringing up the child of a samurai. From the time of infancy one should encourage bravery and avoid trivially frightening or teasing the child. If a person is affected by cowardice as a child, it remains a lifetime scar. It is a mistake for parents to thoughtlessly make their children dread lightning, or to have them not go into dark places, or to tell them frightening things in order to stop them from crying.

In Europe, aspiring knights were required to follow a formal initiation process that culminated with their sovereign dubbing them. By contrast no such process existed in Japan; instead samurai were trained from birth for the station they would hold. Unlike their European cousins, they were not put in the care of friends or relatives for training: it was all done at home.

Sometime between the young warrior-to-be's thirteenth and fifteenth birthday, he underwent a ceremony called alternately *genpuku* or *genbuku*. For the sons of the noble families, this often preceded his first battle.

The genpuku was the coming-of-age. It marked the first time the boy's hair was cut in the manner of an adult: his head was completely shaven and he was given an adult's topknot. He was also given an adult's cap. In some cases, more often when a clan was at war, the cap was replaced with a suit of armour.

For women of the samurai families, at least the more senior, the ceremony was called the *mogi*. This also marked the first time their eyebrows were shaved and their teeth blackened. The latter, through the application of iron oxide, was an ancient court tradition for upper-class women. It also meant that they were ready to marry, often to cement a family alliance.

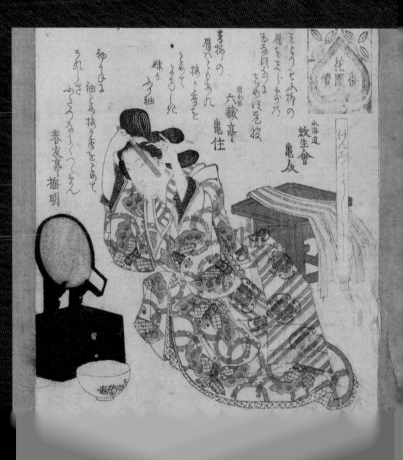

The coming of age ceremony marked the transition from childhood to adult dress and appearance. This print by Hokkei Toyota, entitled '*Genpuku Yoshi*' ('*It's good to become an adult*'), shows a woman on a lucky day for shaving her eyebrows. Shaving the eyebrows and painting them on, and blackening the teeth, were signifiers of transition to adulthood for samurai women. (Library of Congress, Washington)

For the boy children of the samurai, training for their martial way of life began early; from birth if the child showed the unfortunate trait of left-handedness. In Japan, where conformity was paramount, everyone was right-handed: being left-handed was unacceptable. The left arm was tied down, things were placed in the reach of the right hand, everything possible was done to break the habit.

Particularly between the ages of 7 and 8 the boys were encouraged to be sociable and cooperative with their playmates, and discouraged from being confrontational or overly self-absorbed. At 9 and 10, they concentrated on more academic subjects such as reading and writing, although from the age of 7 they were likely to be studying regularly at temple school.

The serious work took place between the ages of 10 and 12, when the child's day could include as many as 12 hours of work in subjects ranging from abstract academics to learning musical instruments or undergoing physical training.

By the time he was 13, he was ready to fight: more than one famous daimyo fought in his first engagement at this age. These young samurai probably gathered around their campfires at night and listened in awe – in the manner of all new recruits – to the stories told by the more experienced campaigners. This in itself was training.

DRESS AND APPEARANCE

As the elite of a daimyo's fighting force, the samurai were expected to set an example to the lower classes by the dignity of their appearance. It could safely be concluded that a dishevelled or unkempt samurai in any situation other than on a battlefield was a man who was unemployable, unwanted or had abandoned himself to crime or to drink. *Hagakure* tells us in 1710:

The samurai of 50 or 60 years ago would bathe, shave their foreheads, put lotion in their hair, cut their fingernails and toenails, rubbing them with pumice and then with wood sorrel, and without fail pay attention to their personal appearance. It goes without saying that their armour in general was kept free from rust, that it was dusted, shined and arranged.

A samurai's personal pride was apparent from the moment of first contact. When out of armour he would wear fine clothes of a particular traditional design. Above a *kimono*, a garment that resembled a dressing gown, he would wear various types of clothing that reflected the situation in which he found himself. Formal duties in a daimyo's castle demanded the kamishimo, the traditional combination of wide hakama (trousers) and either a formal jacket with shoulders that stuck out like wings, or a looser *haori*. The two parts of the kamishimo were of identical colour and design and bore the daimyo's *mon* (family crest) on the breast and on the back. Tight *kobakama* (breeches) were more informal attire. Thrust into the belt of the hakama were the two swords that were the recognised badge of the privileged samurai class.

Particular care was lavished on the samurai's hair. It would be combed and drawn back into a pigtail which either stuck out behind or was folded forward on itself. It was fashionable to have the front part of the head shaved. When in battle the hair would be let down and tied simply with a *hachimaki* (headband) – hence the illustrations on Japanese prints of battle scenes showing samurai with their hair streaming in the wind. *Hagakure* recommended that samurai should grow moustaches so that their severed heads would not be mistaken for those of women. Full beards were most unusual, and Kato Kiyomasa's penchant for facial hair was remarked upon.

One thing the samurai wore at all times, whether in or out of armour, was a sword, or, more often, two. When indoors, he usually just wore the shorter one. They were

ABOVE The finest and most historic example of a daimyo's *yashiki* (mansion) is the Hiunkaku pavilion. It was built by Toyotomi Hideyoshi and formed part of Fushimi Castle until it was transferred to the Nishi Honganji temple in Kyoto. This is the view from the ornamental pond garden. (Photo by Hideyuki Kamon/Flickr)

thrust edge up through the obi, at the left side. The fittings, including the scabbard and guard, were generally matching, but when one sword and a dirk were worn, there was no great need for uniformity. The right to carry weapons was the badge of a samurai's status and a source of pride. The small dirks that women carried in their obi, usually wrapped in a brocade case, were as much a sign of their position as swords were for the men.

Samurai also carried a fan, and perhaps a supply of soft paper (as we carry tissues) and a small purse. Smaller items like the purse could be secreted in a sleeve, while larger items were thrust into the waist sash or between the front folds of the kimono.

THE SAMURAI'S DOMAIN

Up until 1591, when the Separation Edicts enacted by Toyotomi Hideyoshi achieved a rigid distinction between samurai and farmer, a samurai's daily life would have been conducted between the two poles of the daimyo's castle and the samurai's own estates. The extent to which the samurai was merely an estate manager or an actual worker on the land depended on the resources he possessed, which in turn depended on his prowess in the daimyo's service.

Service to one's lord, either on the battlefield or off it, produced reward, but also increased obligation. To some extent this was an unending progression, because a samurai's wealth was measured in terms of the yield of his rice fields. This figure was then translated into the number of men he was required to supply in the daimyo's service. More lands could be farmed, and more food could be produced to feed one's own followers, so more followers were required when danger threatened. Over time, grants of land were replaced by a rice stipend. The professional samurai would now spend most of his time in the service of his daimyo in the daimyo's own headquarters while his own men worked the fields on his behalf, just as he had once done for the daimyo.

The daimyo's base would be centred on a castle. The latter's role as an economic centre encouraged the growth of *jokamachi* (castle towns), which spread around the castle's walls. Many of modern Japan's prefectural capitals were once the castle towns of daimyo. During the course of the Sengoku Jidai, the Japanese castle evolved from being a simple stockade on top of a mountain – the original *yamashiro* (mountain castle) – to the huge fortresses such Osaka and Himeji, where graceful buildings soared into the sky above massive stone bases. The outer walls of such castles sheltered the buildings, which were virtually barracks, where the samurai lived. The quality of the buildings he occupied depended upon the samurai's rank, as did their location. The closest retainers of the daimyo were settled in the buildings nearest to the centre of the castle, where two key complexes would be found. The first was the keep. This was the heart of the military and defensive function of the castle. It provided a lookout tower and also a place for a last-ditch stand in time of war. The final evolution of the castle keep produced the stunning examples that still exist to this day in places like Hikone and Matsumoto. They are often of four or five storeys in height with graceful tiled roofs, heavy doors and windows and clever defensive elements such as trap doors that act like machicolations, as well as spikes and concealed sally ports.

Because a keep was essentially a military structure, it was unusual for the building to be highly ornamented inside. Instead it would be solidly built with plain decoration and polished wooden floors. Any ostentation in the castle was to be found in the daimyo's yashiki (mansion), which would usually lie in the inner

ABOVE This view is of the classic layout of a samurai's yashiki. The floor area is effectively one large room subdivided using opaque sliding screens or the translucent *shoji* screens. Beyond the outer corridor we can see the garden. The floor is covered with *tatami* (rice straw) mats. This is the yashiki of Kochi Castle.

courtyard beside the keep. This would be the living quarters and administrative area for the daimyo and the samurai who were his closest retainers. The yashiki would be a one-storey building that reflected the unity of style of Japanese architecture. Wooden corridors (in some cases made deliberately noisy to warn of intruders) connected sets of rooms subdivided one from another by sliding screens. The shoji (translucent paper screens) on the outer walls of rooms could be slid back to reveal gardens and ponds, while the inner screens were decorated with pictures of landscapes and animals. Rooms were of various sizes depending upon their intended function, from tiny little spaces for an intimate tea ceremony to large and impressive reception areas. A stage for the performance of the Noh drama might well be included in the yashiki complex.

Inside the rooms furniture was minimal. Low wooden tables or desks, an arm rest, a lamp stand and a sword rack would be all that would normally be visible. Subtle decoration was provided by a *tokonoma*. This was an alcove in the corner of a room where a hanging scroll could be displayed or a flower arrangement placed inside some beautiful pottery vase. Just as in traditional Japanese inns today, bedrooms had no beds. The bedding would be packed away in concealed cupboards and only brought out for sleeping. There was no heating other than the warmth provided by an open fire in the middle of a room, or a box of warm charcoal. A kitchen would occupy a space on the outside of the building. Here food would be prepared over a number of ranges and carried into the living quarters on trays. A bath house provided the best relaxation of all. Toilet facilities were private and heavily guarded, as this was the only place where an assassin might hope to encounter a daimyo on his own.

The further down the social scale a samurai lay, the simpler his accommodation became. His house might have only one room and a tiny kitchen area, but all could expect hygiene and cleanliness in the castle environment. This would also be found out in the countryside. Here the simple samurai's mansion would be a farmhouse thatched with rice straw surrounded by a vegetable patch rather than an ornamental garden. Fish might be drying in the sun, and frogs would croak in the rice fields that occupied every square inch of cultivable land.

FOOD AND DRINK

A samurai was brought up in a tradition that emphasised frugality, and this was reflected in his diet. The late 13th-century chronicle *Azuma Kagami* (*Mirror of the East*) tells us how the first shogun, Minamoto Yoritomo, gave a New Year banquet that consisted of only one course: a bowl of rice and a cup of sake (rice wine). Tokugawa Ieyasu is recorded as reprimanding a retainer who brought him fruit out of season as a special treat, although this may have had more to do with Ieyasu's concern over his personal health.

Most of the time samurai food was sparse and simple, consisting mainly of rice, vegetables, soy bean products, fish, seaweed, salt and fruit, but it was always highly nutritious. Vegetables would be freshly gathered except for certain pickles, of which pickled plums and pickled ginger were very common. Giant radishes and fresh mountain greens, a form of spinach, were popular. Burdock, aubergines, cucumbers, chestnuts, mushrooms and root vegetables were also eaten.

A great deal of use was made of products derived from soy beans. Soy sauce was produced commercially, as was *miso* (fermented soy bean paste) which could be made into soup. Tofu (soy bean curd) was an important protein source. Rice had become a regular part of the samurai's diet in the 14th century, but polished rice was a luxury item. Husked rice was far more common, and this could be augmented by millet

ABOVE In this painted scroll we see a group of samurai enjoying a performance from the Noh theatre. (Yamauchi Shrine, Kochi)

or a mixture called *genmai*, which was husked rice and wheat. Rice could be either boiled in a pan, mixed with vegetables and seaweed, steamed, baked or made into rice cakes. *Mochi*, the most common form of rice cakes, were made from rice flour or a mixture of rice and wheat flour.

The products of hunting, such as wild duck, venison or boar, would occasionally augment the protein intake. Samurai were enthusiastic hunters and enjoyed delicacies such as bears' paws, badger and the crackling from the skin of wild boar. Meat could be preserved by salting and drying in strips. The produce of the sea provided much more for a samurai's table. Every conceivable sea creature was caught and eaten, from shrimps to whales. Horse mackerel, tuna, squid and sea bream all appear on menus in samurai history, with the preferred means of preparation always being *sashimi*, whereby fish was cut into strips and eaten raw with soy sauce and *wasabi* (green horseradish paste). Shellfish, including the delicacy *awabi* (abalone), were much used.

Many different kinds of seaweed were also eaten. *Wakame* gave flavouring to dishes and provided a base for stock. The deep purple *nori*, used nowadays in the preparation of sushi, was another commonly eaten seaweed. Deep-fried tempura, regarded as traditionally Japanese, was introduced by the Portuguese during the 16th century.

At the time of the samurai, tea performed the same function as brewing in Europe: it made water safe to drink. For alcoholic refreshment there was sake, rice wine of considerable potency.

The serving of a meal inside a daimyo's yashiki would be attended by considerable ceremony. The guests would sit on the floor and eat using chopsticks from a low table, either one large table or individual smaller ones.

The meal would be brought to them on a lacquered tray, with each individual dish presented immaculately on a lacquered or pottery vessel. Rice would be taken from a large rice pot and etiquette demanded that one should never pour sake for one's own consumption. A meal in a lowly samurai's barracks would be less exquisite in appearance, but would be attended by the same meticulous etiquette. Hygiene was of a very high standard.

REST AND RELAXATION

Although their primary purpose was to be warriors, samurai did not spend all their time fighting or practising in preparation for battle. There was ample opportunity for rest and relaxation, and several of the samurai most renowned for their martial prowess were also famous for being patrons of the arts. The great swordsman Miyamoto Musashi (1584–1645), for example, was also famous as a practitioner of *sumi-e* (ink painting). The testimony of Hojo Soun (1432–1519) to his sons included the statement that the literary and martial arts were to be practised always, because letters were the left hand and military matters the right hand, so that neither should be neglected.

To some extent these two apparently opposite poles were quite closely connected. The administration of one's domains required much more than an ability to lead men into battle, and it is interesting to note how the activities chosen by samurai when 'off duty' nevertheless reflected the primacy of their martial calling.

For example, a visit to a castle by a travelling *biwa* (Japanese lute) player promised much more than mere entertainment. Such men specialised in retelling through epic

RIGHT This print from the *ukiyo-e* artist Yoshitoshi's 'One Hundred Aspects of the Moon' illustrates the paradox inherent in the world of the warrior. The samurai is playing a biwa, the Japanese lute, but he is also fully armed and ready for action. Note the tigerskin cover of his scabbard and the spare bowstring reel attached to it.

ABOVE The most exquisite form of entertainment that a samurai could pursue was the performance of the Japanese tea ceremony, which had its origins in the complex contemplative world of Zen Buddhism. Here we see the thatched teahouse in the garden of the Kodaiji temple in Kyoto. The room used for the tea ceremony is in the foreground and has a circular window. To its right is the entrance that the host will use. As it is extremely low he has to crouch to enter, thus showing his humility. (Photo by John Weiss/Flickr)

poetry stories such as *Heike Monogatari*, the great *gunkimono* (war tale) that tells of the decline and fall of the Taira clan. A performance inside the inner chambers of a daimyo's yashiki would be an uplifting moral experience for a young samurai, who would hear the stories of the deeds of the samurai of the past. *Hagakure* stressed the correct mental attitude at this time. Inspiration to action was more important than any contemplation:

> There is something to which every young samurai should pay attention. During times of peace when listening to stories of battle, one should never say, 'In facing such a situation what should a person do?' Such words are out of the question. How will a man who has doubts even in his own room achieve anything on the battlefield?

Similar historical and exemplary themes occurred in the plays of the Noh theatre. The actors, dressed in period costume and with amazing masks and headdresses, provided an additional visual experience that would enhance a samurai's education about who he was and where he had come from. The game of go, whereby opposing armies of white stones attempt to surround and capture black stones on a board, was a lesson in strategy, not just a pastime. *Shogi* (Japanese chess) added a tactical dimension that made it into a war game.

Of all the pastimes in which a samurai could indulge none had more lore and tradition associated with it than the performance of the tea ceremony. Tea had originally been introduced to Japan as a means of keeping Zen monks awake for their nocturnal devotions. But in addition to its ubiquity as a beverage, tea drinking developed in this one highly specialised way that encompassed much of what a samurai valued in terms of aesthetic appreciation and sensitivity. *Chado,* the Way of Tea, centred on the drinking of a bowl of green tea with like-minded companions in an artistically pleasing and aesthetically inspiring manner. The ceremony would take place in a tea room, which was often located in a teahouse set within a tea garden. The decor of a teahouse was traditionally very simple and rustic, although Hideyoshi, whose flamboyance in artistic matters was renowned, was known to make use of a tea room where the wooden beams were plated with gold. The guests would enter from the garden and take their places, after which the tea *sensei* (master), who was sometimes the daimyo himself, would join them through a separate door made deliberately low so that the sensei was forced to express his humility by crouching very low. A meal of exquisite design and quality might be served, but the centre of the meeting was always the tea ceremony itself, whereby the sensei boiled the water and served the tea in a strict formality that allowed his guests to appreciate every gesture and factor involved. They would admire the quality of the pottery used in the vessels, the reflection of the seasons in a flower arrangement or a hanging scroll in the tokonoma, the play of light in the garden outside, partially visible through the sliding screens. But most of all they would be enthralled by the motions of the tea master as his hands moved in a '*kata* of tea' that would be reminiscent of the greatest exponent of swordplay.

The political pay-off from the tea ceremony was considerable. Information gathered from guests, political support confirmed by attendance, bonds of comradeship forged by fellow enthusiasts, gifts of priceless tea bowls and many other spin-offs arose from these gatherings. Nor should the socially competitive nature of the tea ceremony be overlooked. The Way of Tea sorted the aesthete from the boor and distinguished the patient man from the over-hasty. It revealed areas of self-control that would stand a samurai in good stead on the battlefield. It exposed his weaknesses under pressure.

ABOVE By means of a Japanese garden a samurai sought to bring nature within the walls of his castle or mansion. This view is of one of the finest existing Japanese gardens at Suizenji in Kumamoto. The conical hill represents Mount Fuji. (Photo by sodai gomi/Flickr)

An interesting characteristic of training in Japan is that despite the importance of formal training, a strong emphasis was also placed on the abstract. Some clans valued this mental training highly, and so recommended the chess-like games go and shogi to train the mind in tactics and strategy. For the lower classes of samurai and the ashigaru, it was considered a useless exercise, so they did not study the games formally. Those from the ranks who learnt such games often did so for more earthly reasons: they regarded go and shogi as pleasant pastimes, and occasionally as a source of extra income when they could find someone willing to bet on the outcome.

What the clans considered valuable for the training of their men often depended on the background of the clan. When one considers that many of the great houses of the 16th century were not aristocratic and high-born (rather, they had fought their way to the top from the lower ranks of families), it is clear that they would have had different values from those of the older aristocrats.

The older clans had appreciation for the arts, and encouraged familiarity with them amongst their retainers. This included such things as playing games, composing poetry, playing musical instruments and so on. The newly risen clans in general abhorred such soft and decadent pastimes in favour of strictly martial techniques and exercises. These clan lords often laid down harsh penalties – ranging from demotion or loss of privileges to the extremes of banishment or death – for samurai found to be gambling, attending plays or similarly 'wasting their time'.

Kakun (household rules given at the hands of the daimyo to be used in governing their clans) mark these differences of opinion clearly. The disagreement on the importance of letters (*bun*) and the military (*bu*) was called *bunbu ichi*, or 'supremacy of letters (i.e., things artistic) or martial'. Apparent contradictions in collections of kakun can be striking and include such rules as 'clan members shall not play go or attend theatre, nor shall they learn to play the flute or write poetry' and 'everyone should learn calligraphy because it is good for the mind'

Hagakure, a collection of anecdotes and maxims from the Nabeshima family, is delightfully snobbish in its rejection of alternative beliefs and practices:

The saying, 'the arts aid the body', is for samurai of other regions. For the samurai of the Nabeshima clan the arts bring ruin to the body. In all cases the person who practises an art is an artist, not a samurai.

In the tea ceremony a samurai practised the inner martial arts where he had no sword but his wits, and no defence to a challenge but to draw on the fund of aesthetic knowledge he was required to possess.

A lesser-known pursuit of the samurai class, and one that had little connection to the martial arts, was the curious *kemari* (courtly football), an ancient game originally introduced from China that had been popular among court aristocrats in the Nara and Heian periods. Oda Nobunaga (1534–82) was particularly fond of kemari, and there are several references to games in his contemporary biography. The game was non-competitive and involved passing the ball from one player to another and keeping it in the air. The ball, about eight inches in diameter, was made of deerskin and stuffed with sawdust. There could be a varying number of players, usually between two and eight. There was no tackling. When a player received the ball he was allowed to kick it in the air as many times as he liked in order to show his skill, shouting *'Ariya'* every time he tapped it. Then he would pass the ball to another player with the cry *'Ari!'*. Kemari was played on a pitch called a *kikutsubo* that was marked out by trees. The Heian aristocrats would grow trees in specific areas in their gardens so as to have a permanent pitch. Others grew trees in pots so that they could mark out the pitch in a way dependent on the number of people playing. The four trees used to mark out the pitch were normally a cherry tree, a maple, a willow and a pine.

There were simpler pursuits as well, of course. The more literate samurai composed poetry or whiled away their time in innocent pastimes such as 'guessing the incense' or tea tasting. Stronger beverages provided a more boisterous outlet, and drinking dens flourished in castle towns. Prostitutes were readily available and a welcome relief for samurai hundreds of miles away from home.

BELIEF AND BELONGING: SHINTO, SECTS AND SACRED WARFARE

The samurai was brought up in a world in which religion was all-pervading. Prayers were offered at the start of battles and banners were emblazoned with invocations of the gods of war, who were believed to take part in a righteous cause. On several occasions during the 1592–98 invasion of Korea a Japanese victory was ascribed to the intervention of supernatural forces. If a defeat ensued, blame could be directed towards the anger of the gods.

Zen Buddhism was noted previously as a major influence on the tea ceremony, but this was just one sect among one of Japan's 'five formative traditions' (Shinto, Buddhism, Confucianism, Taoism and folk religion) that have intermingled over the centuries to produce a system that can be understood as an entity. Not only did the various religions mingle, but Japanese people have always participated in rituals from a number of different traditions. The one exception was Christianity, introduced by St Francis Xavier in 1549, and this attitude was partly to blame for its persecution. The willingness to accept different traditions is also recognisable in the attitude that Japanese religion is as much about doing as about believing. It has a strong ritual basis, which was not separated from everyday life in traditional Japan. There were rituals for planting rice and rituals for harvesting it, as well as a host of other activities. In such ways the samurai, particularly those who still farmed on a part-time basis, remained close to the passing of the seasons and their religious roots.

Shinto was the name given during the 19th century to the indigenous religious beliefs of Japan that centred around the worship of a huge number of kami (deities), who were enshrined in shrines known as *jinja*, easily recognisable by the presence at their entrance of the characteristic *torii* (gateway). The Japanese have historically

ABOVE Three priests are rowed ashore in secret to minister to Japanese Christians. By an edict of Tokugawa Ieyasu in 1614, all foreign priests were expelled from Japan.

ABOVE Atsuta Shrine, traditional home of *Kusanagi no tsurugi*, the sword of the Japanese imperial regalia. (Photo by the.Firebottle/Flickr)

been quite content to do without precise conceptions of what kami are, the vagueness expressing something of true kami nature, a concept totally contrary to Western thought. Some kami are, however, quite precisely defined. Emperor Ojin, who reigned during the 3rd century AD, was deified as Hachiman, the kami of war, whose veneration was associated strongly with the Minamoto family.

Samurai would not attend weekly religious services in temples and shrines. Instead, like Japanese people nowadays, they would visit a shrine when they had a need for prayer, such as at departure for war. When Oda Nobunaga set out on the march that led to his victory at Okehazama in 1560, he wrote a prayer for victory and deposited it at the great Atsuta Shrine near present-day Nagoya. The kami would then be expected to aid him in his coming campaign. Rewards would be forthcoming if they did, and retribution in the form of burning a shrine was not unknown when prayers for victory were not answered.

Buddhism came to Japan by way of China in the middle of the 6th century AD. It was a profoundly different religious system, but Shinto and Buddhism became so intertwined that the samurai of the Sengoku Jidai would have recognised little difference between the two, each of which made its own contribution to the religious milieu along with the other traditions. For example, from Shinto came a stress on purification and the avoidance of pollution, which causes offence to the kami. Death in battle required Shinto ceremonies to purify the site, as at the battle of Miyajima in 1555, which was fought on an island that was itself regarded as a Shinto shrine. A samurai's funeral, however, would be conducted according to Buddhist rites in the family temple.

By the time of the samurai, Japanese Buddhism existed as a number of different sects, and although much is made nowadays of the dominant influence of Zen Buddhism, a samurai of the Sengoku Jidai would be every bit as likely to belong to another sect. The original Nara sects tended to come under the patronage of the imperial court, while the Tendai and Shingon sects were esoteric in their approach. Their monks undertook arduous mountain pilgrimages and performed long mysterious rituals in their temples. Their centres were the holy mountains of Hieizan and Koyasan respectively and were associated with warrior monks rather than with the samurai class.

The populist sects of Jodo and Jodo Shinshu, again associated with a link between religious belief and military activity, had numerous members among the samurai class. The latter drew in lower-ranking samurai through their tradition of the formation of *ikki*, associations created by low-ranking samurai families for mutual protection, which could cause serious conflicts of interest when a samurai was also a daimyo's vassal. A prime example was the situation that faced the young Tokugawa Ieyasu in the early 1560s. The Ikko-ikki of Mikawa Province were among his greatest rivals, but several of his retainers were *monto* ('believers') who embraced the Buddhist sect of Jodo Shinshu and had various ties to its community. When issues of armed conflict arose, such men were placed in a quandary. For example, in its account of the battle of Azukizaka in 1564, the *Mikawa go Fudoki*, which records the ancestry of the Tokugawa clan, states:

> Tsuchiya Chokichi was of the monto faction, but when he saw his lord hard pressed he shouted to his companions, 'Our lord is in a critical position with his small band. I will not lift a spear against him, though I go to the most unpleasant sorts of hells!' and he turned against his own party and fought fiercely until he fell dead.

The Nichiren or Lotus sect attracted several famous samurai including Kato Kiyomasa (1562–1611), who emblazoned the sect's motto on his banner. Nichiren, named after its founder, expressed a form of fanaticism akin to that of Jodo Shinshu's Ikko-ikki. Zen, by contrast, presented an image of detachment from the world and the achievement of enlightenment within oneself. The elements of detachment and separation had obvious resonances for a samurai who was going into battle and might not return, so it is worth noting that Zen's other influence on the samurai lay through the performance of the tea ceremony and the enjoyment of a garden. The tea ceremony also had overtones of Taoism, where the emphasis was on 'the way' of doing things, a concept also paramount in understanding the martial arts and their later expression as bushido, the 'way of the warrior'.

CONFUCIANISM, ZEN AND THE SWORD

Confucianism, along with Zen Buddhism, was one of the main philosophical influences on the samurai. The adoption of Confucian ethics provided the model for the relationship between master and follower and ultimately for the Tokugawa shogunate, because Confucianism valued an ordered society where everyone knew his place. In Confucian eyes good government was based on virtue and example rather than on sheer military might. The most important ethical demands made by Confucianism were *ko* (filial piety) and *chu* (loyalty), both of which were fundamental to the ideals of the samurai. Another strong influence was the stress laid by certain Confucian scholars on the necessity to act and the primacy of action over thought. This laid the basis for the fanaticism that was to characterise much samurai behaviour at the time of the transition to modern Japan.

In applying Confucianism to swordsmanship the approach was to stress the ethical meaning of sword fighting, linking prowess in swordsmanship with the warrior's need to serve his master. Here Confucianism met that other great philosophical influence on samurai: the self-denying Buddhism of the Zen sect. Zen Buddhism related

Another warrior tradition in Japan was that of the sohei (literally 'priest warrior'), most often called warrior monks. The word refers originally to the armies maintained by the monasteries of Mount Hiei and Nara from about AD 970. Unlike the samurai, their loyalty was not to the emperor, a clan leader or a daimyo, but to their temple and to the particular sect of Buddhism to which they belonged. The most famous of these was the loyal companion of Minamoto Yoshitsune, the warrior monk Benkei, who fought at the battles of Ichinotani, Yashima and Dannoura in the 1180s.

By the time of the Period of Warring States, however, the original sohei had been joined by other armies who shared a similar commitment to a sacred authority rather than a secular one. These were the armies of the Jodo Shinshu sect, known as the Ikko-ikki (the 'Single-minded League'). The populist Jodo Shinshu communities were very different from the monastic ones of the sohei, and to describe the monto of Jodo Shinshu as 'warrior monks' is somewhat misleading. Their communities attracted samurai, farmers and townsmen in communities of shared religious beliefs led by ordained priests. In fact the teachings of Shinran (1173–1262) with whom the sect originated, had revolutionised Japanese Buddhism by doing away with the duality of monasticism and laity and replacing it with a new emphasis on spiritual egalitarianism.

From the early Sengoku Jidai period these militant Buddhist armies, largely recruited from peasants, had become something of a third force in Japanese politics and were a persistent thorn in the side of Oda Nobunaga. They became so powerful in Kaga Province in the late 15th century that they overthrew the local daimyo and ruled the province for the next 100 years. Their 'fortified cathedrals' at Nagashima and Ishiyama Honganji rivalled any samurai castle and the latter withstood the longest siege in Japanese history. This was a long and bitter campaign directed against a massive castle complex of the latest style situated within a maze of reed beds and creeks. The Ikko-ikki had powerful allies, and supplies were run to them by sea, courtesy of the Mori family, supplies and large numbers of arquebuses were run to them by sea, courtesy of the Mori family. Their satellite fortress of Nagashima also held out for years, and was finally reduced when Nobunaga piled up dry brushwood against the outer walls and burned them all to death.

Although the greatly weakened Ikko-ikki later fought alongside Toyotomi Hideyoshi, they neve

In this plate we see the culmination in 1574 of Oda Nobunaga's long campaign against the Ikko-ikki of Nagashima. The main defensive elements of swamps and reed beds have been breached, and flames from piled up bundles of wood are starting to lick at the outer walls of Nagashima, which is shown as a predominantly wooden structure of palisades, fences and watchtowers. (Peter Dennis © Osprey Publishing)

regained their former political power. In 1602 Tokugawa Ieyasu solved the problem once and for all by founding a new head temple to rival the one built

by Hideyoshi in 1591. The sect was left as a strong religious organisation but was never again capable of being revived as the formidable army of the Ikko-ikki

swordsmanship directly to the Buddhist goals of attaining enlightenment and moving towards the achievement of selflessness. By the blending of self and weapon through action, the swordsman moved towards the goal of complete emptiness which was the aim of all Zen practices.

Much has been made of the links between Zen and swordsmanship. In fact swordsmanship was the possession of no one philosophical system, and to Confucianism and Zen can be added the influence of the ancient Chinese classics, all of which came together to give the 'way of the sword', and with it the 'way of the warrior'.

MEMORY AND ANCESTRY

The most important way in which Japanese folk practices were expressed by samurai was through the significance they placed on the preservation of the memory of their ancestors. Through ancestor veneration the structure of social relationships within a samurai's family unit was extended to encompass the dead. This continuity was assured by a complex series of rituals designed to keep the ancestors peaceful and content in the successive stages through which they would pass. The samurai had the greatest respect for the deeds of his forebears on the battlefield, and these ancestors provided both a model and a source of inspiration.

In early Japan, however, the dead were treated with a mixture of fear and respect. The corpse was a major source of ritual pollution and required Shinto rites of purification, but the spirit of the dead person was also frightening, as it could linger in the realm of the living. These spirits of the dead were venerated and, to some extent, manipulated, along the journey they had to take in order to become an ancestral kami. The process was carried out through the rituals of Buddhism, and may be summarised as follows.

The *shirei* (spirit of the recently dead) became a *hotoke* (an enlightened one). After a period of years there was a transformation to *senzo* (ancestor) and finally to a kami, as part of the collective spirits of the locality. These ancestral kami remained eternally in the land, and continued to work for its prosperity and that of the samurai family. This process was regarded as continuing as long as there was living memory within the family, otherwise it was lost, and the ancestral kami then had to be treated as a collectivity. There was, however, a class of wandering spirits known as *muenbotoke* (Buddhas of no affiliation), who either had no descendants to worship them, or were victims of violent or untimely death, and thus 'remain possessed by the worldly passion in which they died'. It was spirits such as these, often dead samurai slaughtered on battlefields, who provided the rich material for the numerous ghost stories and plays that made up the Noh dramas that many samurai must have enjoyed with a shudder.

BUSHIDO: THE SAMURAI CODE

Just as Shinto means 'the way of the gods', so does the well-known word bushido mean 'the way of the warrior'. There is a strange parallel between the emergence of the two terms. The word Shinto was introduced to provide a label for something that had been going on for centuries and had required no name until it was felt necessary to distinguish it from something else. Scholars are divided as to whether this happened when Buddhism was introduced, or when the founding fathers of the Meiji government sought to create a new ideology. Bushido has a similarly confusing genesis. No event was more important to its creation, development and dissemination than the publication as late as 1905 of a book called *Bushido: The Soul of Japan*, written in English by Inazo Nitobe. It carries the subtitle *An Exposition of Japanese Thought*, and is widely regarded as a classic. As attested by its long catalogue of reprints, its translation into numerous languages and its enthusiastic reception by Westerners and Japanese alike, no book has been more influential in making the ideas and ideals of 'the way of the warrior' accessible to the outside world.

Bushido: The Soul of Japan is a very curious work. Its author was born in 1863, but was shielded from the turbulence of the Meiji Restoration, first by the education he received in schools where the main medium of teaching was in English, then by the Christianity he espoused and to which he remained dedicated all his life, and finally through a certain physical isolation in Hokkaido. The result was a highly literate scholar with a keen sense of internationalisation, whose immersion in a Western education of the English public school variety (often referred to as 'muscular Christianity') was equalled only by his stunning lack of knowledge of Japanese culture. This would not have mattered had he not produced a book about Japan that was to become an international bestseller outside Japan and a cornerstone of right-wing nationalism within it. Although he willingly admitted his ignorance of vital topics such as Zen Buddhism ('so far as I understand it …'), Nitobe's book, with its strange blend of samurai myths and *Tom Brown's Schooldays,* became regarded as the bible of bushido.

Central to Nitobe's presentation of bushido as the 'warrior's code' is his identification of seven key values: justice, courage, benevolence, politeness, veracity, honour and loyalty. In the same way that critics of Shinto's official line of history readily acknowledge the pre-existence of kami worship, so it must be recognised that all these virtues were present in Japan in pre-Meiji times. All indeed are splendid ideals that would first

RIGHT The reality of bushido lay not in any seeking of death, but in the relationship of service between a samurai and his master, as seen in this scroll in Matsuyama Castle.

have graced the halls of a daimyo's castle and then transformed his sword-wielding samurai into brush-wielding exemplars of Tokugawa society. Where Nitobe exceeded his brief was to assume that they made up a rigid 'warrior's code' called bushido. Nitobe presents bushido as a code that was ancient and universally adhered to by the samurai, who effectively swore to obey it like a version of the Hippocratic oath. Such was the popularity of Nitobe's work that not only was all this fully accepted, but his other misconception – that bushido was a moral force that had become in modern times 'the soul of Japan' – became true by default as a self-fulfilling prophecy. In an age that actively sought fundamental values for a rapidly changing society, Nitobe's thesis was exactly what early 20th-century Japan wanted to hear.

Prior to Nitobe, a wide range of expressions – all meaning 'the way of the warrior' – may be found in the literature, such as *shido* and *budo* (the first syllables are the same as in bushido). But where the actual term bushido appears the meaning is always that of a general attitude rather than a rigid accepted code known to all. Nitobe's book does, however, make it clear that bushido was less concerned with the individual samurai than with the relationships the samurai had with others, of which the most important was that between master and follower. One of the finest expressions of this relationship comes from Torii Mototada, who wrote a last letter to his son in 1600 prior to the fall of Fushimi Castle, which he had defended so valiantly for Tokugawa Ieyasu:

> For myself, I am resolved to make a stand inside the castle, and to die a quick death. It would
> not be difficult to break through the enemy and escape … But that is not the true meaning of

RIGHT Single combat with swords: the ideal role of every samurai, but not one that was often performed, even during times of war.

being a warrior, and it would be difficult to account as loyalty … to show one's enemy one's weakness is not within the family traditions of my master Ieyasu. It is not the way of the warrior to be shamed and avoid death even under circumstances that are not particularly important. It goes without saying that to sacrifice one's life for one's master is an unchanging principle.

Torii Mototada sees his conduct as being in keeping with the tradition of service to the ideals of the Tokugawa family, rather than being driven by a code. He goes on to remind his son of their family and its relationship with the Tokugawa, referring to the 'benevolence' of their lord and the 'blessings' they had received at his hands. It is this relationship that is the key to his behaviour, not some abstract philosophical principle.

That Torii Mototada's master recognised his own obligation in giving benevolence is shown by the document that the first Tokugawa shogun left for the instruction of his followers. The *Toshogu goikun*, effectively 'The Testament of Tokugawa Ieyasu', was first published during the reign of his grandson, the third Tokugawa shogun, Iemitsu. In language curiously reminiscent of the Chinese concept of the Mandate of Heaven, the Tokugawa had been divinely entrusted with ruling Japan in the way of heaven (*tendo*), but if that rule were exercised badly, the mandate could be withdrawn. To Ieyasu the 'way of the warrior' had been since ancient times the means by which the shogun had purified the realm of evil. The quality of chu (loyalty) was the virtue required of inferiors, while their leaders responded with *jihi* (benevolence), which was the hallmark of a peaceful and just government. In a curious analogy made with the Japanese imperial regalia, the three cardinal virtues in achieving a harmonious outcome were wisdom, the principle of the mirror; benevolence, the principle of the sword; and straightforwardness, the principle of the jewel.

THE MARTIAL ARTS

The samurai existed as a fighting man, so much of his time had to be given to increasing his prowess in fighting techniques. These skills gave rise to the modern martial arts of Japan, so *kenjutsu* (sword techniques), for example, became modern *kendo* (literally 'the way of the sword'). Schools of swordsmanship were developed during the Period of Warring States. They were led by experts known by the title of sensei, a word that can be translated simply as 'teacher', but implies such a tremendous respect verging on awe that the word 'master' gives a better idea of its meaning.

The mythology and mystique that has grown up over the centuries around the martial arts of Japan has tended to lay too great a stress on the transmission from master to pupil of secret techniques. The author of *Hagakure* recognised this trend at the end of the 17th century, when he writes of a dying sensei, who told his best disciple:

> I have passed on to you all the secret techniques of this school, and there is nothing left to say. If you think of taking on a disciple yourself, then you should practise diligently with the bamboo sword every day. Superiority is not just a matter of secret techniques.

No matter how skilled a sensei was, he was hampered by one inescapable fact: realistic practice with such a deadly weapon as a samurai sword was almost impossible. The slightest mistake by one of a pair of sparring students would have led to death, so various teaching methods were developed in response. The usual scheme was for an aspiring student to learn first of all the basic techniques. If no opponent was involved, this could be done with real swords. The student would move on to set techniques using a practice sword and an opponent, followed by using a *habiki* (edgeless sword), a real sword with a completely blunt blade. The final stage involved the use of an edged weapon.

ABOVE Prowess at swordsmanship required endless practice in a dojo with real weapons, blunted swords or wooden practice swords. Here a sensei is taking on a promising pupil. Both are dressed in practical kimono and hakama, but the pupil has fastened back the sleeves of his kimono and has his hair tied back in 'tea whisk' style. The bandages on the other pupils show that quite severe blows could be sustained using the practice weapons shown in the corner behind them. (Angus McBride © Osprey Publishing)

One variety of practice in the first stage was *suburi*, a drilling method whereby the sword was swung over and over against an imaginary opponent. Although similar to shadow-boxing, suburi had real value in that it taught the samurai good balance with a real weapon and developed his muscles. A student could also perform kata, a standard practice method still found in Japanese martial arts today, which is the performance of set moves or forms in a precise and prescribed manner. The student could also practise kata with a partner. In this case each knew precisely what the other's next move would be, so real swords were an option. Like suburi, the repetitious kata could become boring, and required great dedication from the student. But in the Period of Warring States the prize was not a gold medal in a competition: it was survival on a battlefield and the achievement of the simple goal of doing one's duty to the daimyo, and that, theoretically at any rate, was all that the samurai lived for.

The substitution of dummy weapons for real ones allowed a certain amount of contact between opponents. For *yarijutsu* (spear techniques) the samurai used a *tampo yari*, a practice spear with a round padded end, and for sword fighting they used *bokuto*. The word bokuto consists of the two characters for 'wood' and for 'sword', as that is what bokuto were: wooden swords made with the overall shape of a real sword and with a real sword's approximate weight. To compensate for the higher density of steel, the blade was made about an inch thick, and was practically identical to the modern bokuto, also called *bokken*, used in present-day aikido. Samurai fighting with bokuto would not wear protective armour but fought instead with unmasked faces and unprotected sleeves. The result was that even if mortal wounds and disablement were avoided, very savage blows could still be sustained leading to severe bruising and the occasional broken limb.

Towards the end of the 16th century a new practice weapon called a *shinai* was introduced and was developed for friendly encounters. The original shinai, almost identical to the weapon used in modern kendo, consisted of a number of light bamboo blades tied together. If some form of protective armour was worn, blows could be delivered with the light shinai using all the power in a samurai's forearms, and enabling what one might term 'full-contact kenjutsu' to be practised, thus making a simulation of actual combat more realistic. It was introduced by the sensei Kamiizumi Nobutsuna, and first used by him in a duel against Yagyu Muneyoshi. A century later, about 1711–14, the sensei Chosho Shiroemon began to use protection for the face and forearms similar to modern kendo armour for practising the martial arts, but shinai and armour were always abandoned for serious contests and bokuto used instead. The samurai swordsman of the Sengoku Jidai had to be tough as well as skilful, so a few bruises were fully acceptable. The third stage of training using blunted swords must have caused even more physical damage.

Bokuto were also used for duels between rivals and it was the accepted practice that before two men began such a fight, they exchanged documents which said that neither cared for mortal wounds. In some contests the fighters would use a method of pulling their punches before the opponent was actually struck, thus giving one a victory 'on points'. This technique, also used in sword practice sessions, was called *tsumeru*. To be praised for one's tsumeru, especially in the heat of a contest, was one of the greatest compliments a swordsman could receive. This was, however, always difficult to achieve, and it was equally difficult to judge when a victory had been gained in the split second that the decisive blow was laid. This is very well illustrated in a famous scene in the film *Seven Samurai*. The duel is based on an incident that

RIGHT Women of the samurai class were trained in the martial arts to prepare them for the eventuality of having to defend themselves and their families. In this print by Toyokuni we see two women dressed in the costume of the later Edo Period practising with bokuto, the dummy wooden swords used by samurai to enable 'full-contact' sword practice.

MIYAMOTO MUSASHI (1584–1645)

The swordsman as artist is best exemplified by the strange figure of Miyamoto Musashi, a ronin and expert swordsman who seems to have spent many years wandering and engaging in duels. His story has been so obscured by legend that it is difficult to disentangle the man from the myth, but he is believed to have been undefeated in 60 such single combats, and was famous also for his two-weapon fighting style, using a katana and the shorter *wakizashi* sword together. He comes over as a peculiar character, solitary and obsessive, whose skills with the sword are unquestioned and greatly admired, but which at the same time make him feared and disliked. His life consisted of a series of wanderings, short periods in the service of various daimyo, numerous duels and an increasingly deep philosophical insight into swordsmanship, taking its final form in the famous *Gorinsho* (*Book of Five Rings*) which he completed shortly before his death. Miyamoto Musashi made an outstanding contribution to the literature surrounding swordfighting. He was also a skilled painter and calligrapher, and ink paintings by him are much admired as examples of Zen-inspired art. Miyamoto Musashi also respected the sword for its own artistic merits, a trait he held in common with most of his contemporaries.

This hanging scroll from Shimada Art Museum in Kumamoto shows the famous and enigmatic Miyamoto Musashi in characteristic pose armed with a sword in each hand. Musashi was renowned for his ability to wield a katana and a wakizashi at the same time.

is supposed to have occurred in the career of the swordsman Yagyu Mitsuyoshi. The supposed loser in a fight with dummy swords was so convinced he had won that he made his opponent fight again with real swords. His rival, convinced of his own superiority, was reluctant to agree, and only fought with real swords when his opponent started to goad him. Mitsuyoshi's skills were demonstrated beyond any doubt when he killed the man in the process.

Tsumeru techniques were of course the only acceptable form of 'full contact' when the final stage of a swordsman's training using real swords was reached. Tsumeru was brought to perfection by Miyamoto Musashi in the early 17th century, who was an expert at tsumeru with real swords. According to one of the many stories told about him, he could so perfectly control the blow from a katana (samurai sword) that he could sever a grain of rice placed on a man's forehead without drawing blood. Such self-control would establish a swordsman's skills beyond any doubt, but for lesser mortals sword practice in the Sengoku Jidai with dummy swords did lead to some rather odd-looking and unsatisfying contests. The need to avoid death or injury also placed the sensei in a quandary when it came to assessing their pupils' progress.

Prowess at tsumeru with real swords was probably the best guide to a budding samurai's attainment, but his entire mental and physical attitude would be under review, and an experienced sensei knew exactly what to look for.

There was one way in which a samurai could practise some of his swordsmanship skills in a real-life situation. This was by the execution of criminals. In *Hagakure* Yamamoto Tsunetomo records, 'Last year I went to the Kase Execution Grounds to try my hand at beheading, and I found it to be an extremely good feeling.' Formerly, he tells us, all the young samurai were expected to have carried out a beheading by the age of about 15, and even 5-year-olds could use swords to kill dogs. A more merciful alternative was to hack at bundles of bamboo or tatami (rice-straw) mats.

The above techniques presupposed a situation where both opponents had drawn their swords and were squarely facing each other safely out of striking distance. But there was another set of sword techniques that laid the emphasis on drawing the sword and cutting in a single stroke. This was *iai*, whereby a series of moves were practised time and again to allow a samurai to draw the sword from his scabbard and deliver a deadly blow all in one rapid movement.

Practice with missile weapons allowed far freer range and more realistic simulation of battle situations. Hours would be spent at ranges loosing arrows and firing guns. The sublime skill of horseback archery could be honed by the practice of *yabusame*, the colourful sport still demonstrated at shrine festivals today. Dressed in hunting gear, the samurai would loose arrows from a galloping horse against a small wooden target. Practice in shooting at moving targets could be provided by shooting dogs, a speciality of the Hojo family that drew scorn from Toyotomi Hideyoshi in 1590 when he confronted them with firearms.

Spear techniques from the saddle must have been practised, but there is a dearth of references as to how this was done. The nearest form of martial art to equestrian yarijutsu appears to be *dakyu*. This was the Japanese equivalent of polo, and is said to have the same roots in Central Asia. Dakyu was played between two teams of five riders. There was only one goal post, on which either red or white flags were raised when a team scored a goal. The game concluded when 12 balls had been played. Although popular in the Nara Period, dakyu went into a decline until being revived by the shogun Tokugawa Yoshimune (1677–1751) who was an enthusiast for the martial arts. Dakyu riders wielded a long pole with a net at the end, making the action more like mounted lacrosse than Western polo, but the benefits for training a mounted samurai are obvious.

千代田之御表
（埴懐之
山覚）

ABOVE The first samurai were mounted archers, and it was by his skill in loosing arrows from horseback that a warrior's prowess was judged. The technique was practised endlessly and gave rise to the colourful martial art of yabusame, whereby mounted archers dressed in hunting costume try to hit wooden targets at the gallop. Yabusame may still be seen in Japan today at festivals.

ARMS AND ARMOUR

SAMURAI WEAPONRY

The samurai is probably the only warrior in history whose traditional weapon is as well known as the warrior himself. The Gurkhas may be renowned for their kukris and the Vikings for their broad axes, but there is no more celebrated union of warrior and weapon than the samurai and his sword. Forged by master craftsmen to a standard of metallurgy that contemporary Europe can only have dreamed of, the samurai sword was the deadliest of weapons, the most cherished of possessions and, in the words of Tokugawa Ieyasu, nothing less than the 'soul of the samurai'.

It is therefore somewhat sobering to find that in the harsh reality of samurai warfare the Japanese sword was never that highly regarded. All samurai carried swords and used them to good effect, but in battle no samurai ever relied solely on them. Nor were all swords of the superlative quality that traditional views would have us believe. Broken blades are frequently reported, and a samurai could also be put at a disadvantage when his sword got stuck in the body of an opponent that he had just killed. One warrior is recorded uttering a prayer that his sword might be dislodged from his enemy's corpse. There are very few exclusive references in *Heike Monogatari*

LEFT A participant in the *Jidai Matsuri* ('Festival of the Ages') in Tokyo wearing colourful armour and the traditional pair of swords. (Photo by *Danita Delimont*/Gallo Images/Getty Images)

ABOVE In this vivid print about one of Takeda Shingen's victories we see an excellent example of samurai *yari* (spear) techniques from horseback. The rider has transfixed two enemies with his blade. In the background Odai Castle is burning.

to swordplay. Instead the use of the sword is but one stage in a process that begins with the bow, moves through the sword to the dagger and often ends with bare hands.

During the formative years of the samurai tradition the most important weapon was the bow. The first expression that we come across in the earliest war chronicles and epic poetry to describe the samurai's calling makes no reference to a sword. Instead the phrase used is *kyuba no michi,* the 'way of horse and bow'.

The first samurai were mounted archers, and it was by the skill in loosing arrows from horseback that a warrior's prowess was judged. The technique was practised endlessly, and gave rise to the colourful martial art of yabusame, whereby mounted archers tried to hit wooden targets at the gallop.

Historical records give us a fair idea of the efficacy of arrows fired from the Japanese longbow. A direct hit between the eyes that avoided the peak of a samurai's helmet and the facemask would of course be instantly fatal, but it was more common for samurai to die after sustaining multiple arrow hits. This was largely due to the stopping power of their armour, and the popular image from woodblock prints of the dying samurai crawling along like a porcupine with hundreds of arrows protruding from him is not too much of an exaggeration. A certain Imagawa Yorikuni, who fought during the Nanbokucho Wars of the mid–late 12th century, needed 20 arrows to kill him. It was only when the arrows were spent that the mounted archer became a samurai swordsman.

The Sengoku Jidai samurai's *yumi* (bow) was of made from deciduous wood faced with bamboo. The rattan binding reinforced the poor adhesive qualities of the glue used to fasten the sections together and the whole bow was lacquered to weatherproof it. The arrows were of bamboo. The nock was cut just above a node for strength, and three feathers were fitted. Bowstrings were of plant fibre, usually hemp or ramie, coated with wax to give a hard smooth surface, and in some cases the long bow needed more than one person to string it. The archer held the bow above his head to clear the horse, and then moved his hands apart as the bow was brought down to end with the left arm straight and the right hand near the right ear. To release the string the fingers supporting the thumb were relaxed, at which the bow, having discharged the arrow, rotated in the hand so that it ended with the string touching the outside of the bow arm.

As time went by, another consideration began to militate against the samurai being seen as an individual swordsman and nothing else. Armies were growing in size, and the ashigaru had to be armed with the finest weapons that a daimyo could afford. Large numbers inevitably ruled out top quality, leading to one daimyo commenting that if a thousand spears could be purchased for the price of one superlative sword, then it should be the spears that made their way into the samurai armoury. But spears were just one weapon in the ashigaru arsenal. The footsoldiers were also issued with bows, thus destroying forever the image of the samurai as an elite mounted archer.

By the time of the Sengoku Jidai, the occupation of the archer operating from horseback had become limited to those who had sufficient skill to act as mounted sharpshooters. They were still in great demand, because the alternative missile weapon, the arquebus, was not the best thing to operate from horseback. In the mid-16th century we see matchlock pistols being introduced, but again they were of very limited capacity.

RIGHT This panel of a print by Kuniyoshi shows ashigaru (footsoldiers) of the Takeda family at the fourth battle of Kawanakajima in 1561. They are the retainers of Yamamoto Kansuke, who committed suicide when he realised that his battle plans had gone wrong and that the Takeda were heading for certain defeat. The dramatic background of Mount Fuji heightens the tragedy of the scene, because Kansuke's suicide proved to be unnecessary.

ABOVE Ashigaru on the march, showing guns in waterproof cases and naginata.

The yari carried by the mounted samurai bore little resemblance to a European knight's lance. They were lighter and shorter and were not carried in a couched position. Their blades were short and very sharp on both edges, with their tangs sunk into stout oak shafts. This made the yari into a weapon unsuitable for slashing but ideal for stabbing – the best technique to use from a saddle. A useful variation was a cross-bladed spear that enabled a samurai to pull an opponent from his horse. If a samurai wished to deliver slashing strokes from horseback, a better choice than a yari was the cumbersome naginata or the spectacular *nodachi*, an extra-long sword with a very strong and very long handle. Yari would also be the samurai's primary weapon of choice when he had to fight dismounted, and a whole field of martial arts techniques existed for teaching its correct use.

After the spear there was, of course, the famous samurai sword. Much has been written about this legendary weapon, of how its secrets were passed down from master to pupil and of the complex and clever way it was made. Japanese swords could be objects of great beauty, but to the samurai of the Period of Warring States function was more important than form. The finest swords, often presented as gifts to worthy warriors, were of superb finish. They were perfectly balanced for the two-handed style of fighting that they demanded. The samurai never used shields.

Instead the katana, the standard fighting sword, was both sword and shield, its resilience enabling the samurai to deflect a blow aimed at him by knocking the attacking sword to one side with the flat of the blade and then following up with a stroke of his own. The cutting edge was able to take a razor-like quality, while the surrounding body of the sword blade allowed the necessary flexibility to absorb the shock of parrying an enemy's blow. The wavy line running along the blade showed where the two parts of the blade were welded together.

The katana blade would be mounted in a wooden handle bound with silken cords over a layer of *same* (the skin of the giant ray). The scabbard would be lacquered, and often highly decorated, and the whole ensemble was completed with an attractively carved iron *tsuba* (sword guard) and other ornaments. A shorter sword, the wakizashi, joined the katana to make a pair known as a *daisho*, the wearing of which was the badge and exclusive privilege of a samurai. The two swords were sometimes worn while in armour, but it was more usual for the katana to be suspended with its blade downwards from a sword belt and accompanied by a *tanto* (dagger) instead of a wakizashi.

The naginata, a long-bladed polearm, appears prominently on all the painted scrolls of battles that date from the 13th century and earlier. They are better known now perhaps as the traditional weapon of the female warrior, and along with the bow the naginata is the weapon most frequently mentioned as being carried by samurai women. It is also the weapon usually depicted in the hands of Tomoe Gozen, the most famous female warrior, although the account of her last battle from *Heike Monogatari* stresses her accomplishments with bow and sword. So common are the references to naginata in the descriptions of women fighting during the Sengoku Jidai that we must regard a preference for its use as authentic. Certainly by the Tokugawa Period the martial art of naginata was a common pursuit for women of the samurai class.

In appearance the naginata is like a cross between a sword and a spear with a curved blade rather than a straight one. The major difference between a naginata shaft and a spear shaft is that the naginata shaft is of oval cross section so that it may be more easily wielded for cutting rather than thrusting. The curved blade invariably ended in a very sharp point, but it was the considerable momentum of its cutting edge, delivered with the power of the turning shaft behind it, that made the naginata a formidable weapon. The quality of forging required for the blade of a naginata

ABOVE A print depicting Tomoe Gozen, the famous female samurai, and another warrior, possibly Yoshinaka, on horseback. (Library of Congress, Washington)

was in no way inferior to that of a sword, and many famous swordsmiths produced celebrated naginata blades of varying lengths.

Neither spears, naginata, swords nor bows were to be responsible for the military revolution that transformed Japanese warfare during the course of the Sengoku Jidai. This was brought about by the introduction of firearms.

The first guns came to Japan from China in 1510 and consisted of a short iron tube fixed to a long wooden shaft. The barrel was wider around its touch hole and had a slightly conical muzzle terminating in an elongated aperture. Pictures of similar European models show the stock of the gun being held tightly under the left arm while the right hand applied the lighted match. This type of gun is known to have been used in battle as late as 1548 at Uedahara, but it was never widely adopted in Japanese warfare and was immediately scrapped following the dissemination of a much more sophisticated model. This was the arquebus, introduced from Portugal in 1543. Its arrival was unexpected and completely unheralded, being just one very interesting item of exotica possessed by an unfortunate band of Portuguese traders whose wrecked ship was washed up on the Japanese island of Tanegashima in 1543. Tanegashima happened to be owned by the Shimazu of Satsuma, one of the most warlike samurai families in Japan. So when the Portuguese arranged a demonstration of the new weapons the local daimyo saw instantly what a wonderful opportunity had come his way and his most skilled swordsmiths suddenly became gunsmiths. On the most conservative estimate 10 arquebuses were manufactured in Satsuma

LEFT It was not easy to wield the normally two-handed *tachi* from the back of a horse. The one advantage the horseman had was that his superior position would enable him to hit a footsoldier with greater force. On this painted screen a samurai is using his sword like this at the battle of Yashima.

over the following year, although Mendes Pinto, the Portuguese traveller who was much given to exaggeration, put the number at 600. Yet even Pinto was hardly exaggerating when he explained the great popularity of the new weapons as being due to the Japanese 'being naturally addicted to the wars, wherein they take more delight than any other nation we know'.

The arquebus was a simple muzzle-loading musket fired by a lighted match that was dropped onto the pan when the trigger was pulled. It was already revolutionising European warfare, and similar models had helped bring about the victory of the Spanish general Gonzalo de Cordoba at Cerignola in 1503. Gonzalo had been faced with heavily armoured French knights who were used to breaking an enemy position by a fierce frontal charge. At Cerignola, Gonzalo had the privilege of selecting his own position, so he chose to act defensively by digging a ditch, reinforcing it with stakes, and creating a front line in which as many as 2,000 arquebusiers may have been deployed in four ranks. Japan provided no parallel with Cerignola until the battle of Nagashino in 1575, where the Takeda clan took the role of the French at Cerignola and suffered a similar disaster when massed ranks of arquebuses broke their charge.

After Nagashino the use of large numbers of arquebuses became commonplace. As for larger-scale firearms, it is generally believed that the samurai made very little use of cannon or indeed any form of heavy artillery until the last major campaign of the Sengoku Jidai at Osaka between 1614 and 1615.

Notwithstanding their decisive contribution to samurai warfare, firearms of all sizes were received in Japan both as a blessing and a curse. This was exactly the same ambivalent attitude towards them that was being expressed within Europe. Firearms helped a general win battles, but there was a cost that was measured not merely in

ABOVE The battle of Nagashino marked the beginning of the end for the once mighty Takeda clan. This illustration depicts the famous charge by the Takeda on Oda Nobunaga's arquebusier position. Nobunaga had arranged three ranks of arquebusiers to fire in turns from behind a sturdy wooden barricade. Between the barricades were narrow gaps to allow the Oda lancers and cavalry to make sorties from behind their defences. The strategy was a success and the Takeda clan suffered catastrophic losses. (Angus McBride © Osprey Publishing)

文林

men's lives. Honour, pride and personal glory were also placed under threat by these new weapons, whether that pride was possessed by a Spanish knight or a Japanese samurai. The attitude that both cultures had in common was snobbery – such devilish weapons were usually operated by the lower classes of society.

CLOTHING AND BODY ARMOUR

The clothes worn under armour would have been of much simpler design than the samurai's usual dress, although an embroidered *yoroi-hitatare* (armour robe) of a senior samurai would look splendid. On a more mundane level, *Hagakure* recommends underwear made from badger skin, which would eliminate lice infestation, a frequent problem on campaign.

Early Japanese armour was predominately of lamellar construction, in other words it was made from small scales of metal fastened together rather than from one large armour plate. Unlike European armour, the small armour plates were lacquered as a precaution against rust, commonly black, but deep reds and browns were also popular. The individual plates were fastened to each other by rawhide cords to make horizontal sections, a number of which were combined vertically by silk suspensory cords.

Various combinations of plates provided a complete suit of armour. There was a *do* (body armour) from which hung a row of *kusazuri* (tassets) making an armoured skirt. Sleeve armour (*kote*) was worn, as were larger shoulder plates (*sode*)

LEFT Kimura Tsudaro, a late Edo Period *hatamoto* (bannerman) of Nihonmatsu, was killed at the age of 22 during the defence of Nihonmatsu Castle in the Boshin War of 1868. He is shown in the scroll in the Nihonmatsu Museum wearing traditional samurai costume and carrying an arquebus.

THE MAKING OF A JAPANESE SWORD

Detail of Artisans screen from about the 16th century, showing swordsmiths at work. (Photo by Werner Forman/Universal Images Group/Getty Images)

Even though none of the techniques used by the early swordsmiths was apparently ever written down, the smiths' traditions are so strong that even today some superb swords are made using the presumed methodology of a past age. The creation of a fine katana was, and still is, a matter of tradition and religious solemnity. The kami is first invoked before the *tosho* (swordsmith), clad in white priestly robes, begins

transforming the raw materials into a finished product.

Rare *satetsu* (iron sand) would be smelted in small primitive furnaces at 1,300–1,500°C to produce raw steel pieces. The best were beaten into thin cakes, and the expert would select the ones most suitable for swordmaking.

By controlling cooling speed to produce two forms of steel – one exceptionally hard and one softer – and then combining them to make a blade, the Japanese tosho were able to create a weapon with a super-hard cutting edge but also a resilient body that would absorb impacts.

The sections were created and initially treated similarly. First, the pieces of raw steel were heated in the furnace to about 1,300°C, resulting in a basic block of steel. After impurities were removed, the steel was repeatedly heated and beaten, then continuously folded back upon itself so as to create a complex structure with several layers. The steel for the outer skin received the most foldings.

Next, the two separate pieces were combined. Whatever method was used, the outer skin would enclose the core of the sword along its length until just short of the tip. With repeated heating and hammering, the combined steels were slowly drawn out into the rough but recognisable outline of a Japanese blade – at this stage still uncurved. The point (*kissaki*) was then created by cutting off the end of the billet, leaving a triangular shape.

Next the sword back was hammered thicker than the cutting edge, the tang differentiated from the blade and the blade's distinctive curve created. Then came the crucial hardening of the edge. Using a coat of slurry clay to protect all except the cutting edge from the hardening process, the blade was heated to about 730ºC and then plunged into water of a specific (and secret) temperature. The process of tempering allowed the boundary between the two degrees of hardness to be revealed in the edge pattern, called the *hamon*.

The blade was now polished using a succession of finer-grained stones,

Katana, showing the waved edge pattern and the blade.

then whetted and sharpened. The maker would normally inscribe his signature and the date of manufacture on the tang. The finished blade was mounted in a *tsuka* (handle) and a tsuba (guard) protected the hands. A made-to-measure scabbard (*saya*) was created out of magnolia wood. The sword could then be tested on bundles of rushes, corpses or even live condemned criminals.

A tsuba (hand guard) from the Edo period (Rijksmuseum).

and a *nodowa* (throat protector). Beneath the do, *haidate* (thigh guards) and *suneate* (shin guards) provided protection for the legs. The only examples of true plate armour appeared above the neck, where a *menpo* (face mask), often embellished with features and horsehair moustaches, provided a secure anchor point for the heavy iron bowl of the *kabuto* (helmet). A lamellar *shikoro* (neck guard) hung round the helmet's rim, while the helmet's crown was often used to enhance the samurai's martial appearance by the addition of weird and wonderful decorations. Antlers, golden horns, imitation sword blades, rows of feathers and conch shells carved in papier mâché were all to be found transforming a sombre and practical battledress into a glorious fantasy. The popularity of wooden buffalo horns meant that many samurai wore horned helmets.

The samurai's allegiance was proclaimed by the wearing on the back of his armour of an identifying device known as a *sashimono*. This was often, but not exclusively, a small flag bearing his daimyo's mon, but just as in the case of the helmets, the choice of design of the sashimono provided the opportunity for a little creativity. Golden fans and plumes of feathers could replace the small flag, while the most spectacular form of sashimono was the curious *horo*. This was a cloak stretched over a bamboo framework and had supposedly originated as an arrow catcher, but by the time of the Sengoku Jidai it had become a decorative appendage for a daimyo's elite samurai who acted as his bodyguards or messengers. The horo filled with air as the samurai rode across the battlefield, and the bright colours, often with the addition of his daimyo's mon, made him easily recognisable from a distance to friend and foe. There is a reference in the *Hosokawa Yusai Oboegaki* (*The Diary of Hosokawa Yusai*, 1534 –1610) to the elite status of a horo wearer and the following recommendation:

ABOVE In this painted scroll depiction of the battle of Hasedo, the three samurai on the right, hatamoto of Mogami Yoshiaki, pursue their enemies, one of whom is carrying a horo. One of the Mogami samurai has a gohei sashimono and carries a long club, while another has a more conventional flag sashimono and wields a naginata.

When taking the head of a horo warrior wrap it in the silk of the horo, and in the case of an ordinary warrior, wrap it in the silk of the sashimono.

Early armour: the o-yoroi, do-maru and haramaki-do

The *o-yoroi*, which first appeared during the Heian Period and was widely used during the Gempei War, is probably the armour most people associate with the samurai. It is boxy-looking, yet it does what it was designed to do with remarkable efficiency. It was, first and last, armour for the mounted warrior. When the o-yoroi ('great armour') first appeared, warriors of rank fought from horseback and the weapon of choice was the deadly longbow.

O-yoroi armour was made from small scales called *kozane* fastened together. The main body of the armour rigidly protected the trunk by encasing it in four steps of lames, with an additional two boards protecting the chest, and two more for the back. Pendant from it at the front, left side and back were three large tassets called kusazuri which reached to mid-thigh, with rigidly lacquered lames floating loosely on their rows of suspensory braid. The right side of the torso was defended by a solid metal plate called the *waidate*, from which was suspended the fourth kusazuri.

The front of the torso section was covered with a printed leather panel called a *tsurubashiri* ('bowstring running'). Its purpose was to protect both scales and bowstring from each other – the bowstring from snagging, the scales from wear

LEFT This samurai sitting under a cherry tree is wearing a yoroi style of armour with large sode (shoulder guards) and a leather-covered breastplate. He is carrying a bow and wears a courtier's cap. By the time of the Period of Warring States this style of armour was regarded as old-fashioned, but was still worn by generals who wished to identify with their glorious ancestors.

and tear. The designs used for the tsurubashiri ranged from geometrical patterns to illustrations of Shinto and Buddhist deities, dragons and floral patterns. Whichever design was used here was repeated throughout the rest of the armour where leather panels were used (notably the turnbacks on the shikoro, the waidate and covering for the top plates of all the scales).

Also part of the o-yoroi was a pair of large flat shoulder guards called sode (literally 'sleeves'). Their design made them almost resemble squared-off kusazuri. The sode were anchored in place by a series of cords. The sode were made large specifically because the mounted warrior could not handle a bow, control his mount and hold a shield all at the same time.

Hanging from the top of the breastplate and designed to protect the armpits when the arms were in motion were two asymmetrical plates called the *sendan no ita* and *kyubi no ita*.

The *do-maru* (literally 'torso round') was a tighter-fitting armour than the o-yoroi, but also fastened under the right arm. It also had more kusazuri, generally seven, and no leather tsurubashiri chest panel. The do-maru appeared early – during the Nara Period and well before the o-yoroi – but in its earliest incarnations it was still considered a variation of the *keiko*, an earlier, pre-samurai armour type. It had the benefit of being lighter than other armours, and since it fitted closer to the body, it was easier to move and fight in. It was a plainer armour, and as such was deemed unsuitable for warriors of rank; but at about the time of the Gempei War

RIGHT The yoroi armour, with its large sode and four kusazuri, was a beautiful work of art as well as a defence. This example, exhibited in the museum of the Tsurugaoka Hachimangu shrine, may be a modern reconstruction of a Kamakura period armour. (Photo by DeAgostini/Getty Images)

even upper-class samurai began wearing it occasionally, in deference to its comfort and functionality.

Almost identical in style to the do-maru was the *haramaki-do* (literally 'belly-wrap torso'). The only difference was that the closure was up the back, and rather than an overlap there was actually a gap; a separate piece, looking like a section of the cuirass with a single kusazuri, was often worn to cover this opening. This was called a *seita* ('back plate'), but as one should never show the enemy one's back, and therefore should not need such a plate, it was frequently called a 'coward's plate'. This style of armour appeared fairly late, perhaps around the 12th century.

When worn by retainers, the huge sode used with o-yoroi were not part of the do-maru/haramaki-do set. Rather, two plates were hung off the shoulder straps over the edge of the shoulders. These were shaped roughly – at least originally – like apricot leaves, hence the name *gyoyo*. When the do-maru or haramaki-do was worn by men of rank, they would often wear the sode with them, repositioning the gyoyo to hang in front of the armpits as replacements for the sendan no ita and kyubi no ita.

A throat guard called a nodowa was commonly worn under the o-yoroi.

Armour in the Sengoku Jidai

Samurai armour changed very little during the Sengoku Jidai. The main developments were caused by the need to make armour bulletproof once firearms had become established. We therefore see the introduction of solid-plate breastplates for the do, and also solid iron plates for the horizontal sections of skirts and shoulder guards.

LEFT In the Nishimura Museum in Iwakuni we find this excellent example of a multi-coloured armour of haramaki style (opening at the back), which was popular in the Period of Warring States.

This had the additional advantage of saving time for the armour maker, whose craft was in high demand. *Hagakure* adds a few details about armour:

> For soldiers other than officers, if they would test their armour, they should test only the front. Furthermore, while ornamentation on armour is unnecessary, one should be very careful about the appearance of the helmet. It is something that accompanies his head to the enemy's camp.

Old-style armour hung from the shoulders, its full weight supported by the shoulder boards. Around 1450, cuirasses began to taper in at the waist where they could be tightened. What they lost in flexibility, they gained in comfort. This armour, more closely fitting the torso, sat on the hips, and so came to be called *tachi-do*, or 'standing cuirass'.

Along with this development came a slight restructuring of the plates making up the armour. While the older styles invariably had two small breast boards (and three back boards) and four wrapping around the stomach, the modern armour appearing in the mid-16th century began to sport narrower lames. This necessitated three breast boards (with four back boards) and five wrapping lames. This new pattern was the most visible indicator of the *tosei gusoku*, or modern armour. As the modern armour was made with solid plates instead of scale, the reason for the narrower plates is clear: scale armour needed deeper boards to support the large number of holes for lacing; plate lames simply did not need that much depth.

Unlike the gigantic sode of the older armours, the new tosei sode were smaller, narrower, slightly curved and better fitting. As most armour in the last decades

RIGHT Detail of Artisans screen from about the 16th century, showing armourers at work. (Photo by Werner Forman/Universal Images Group/Getty Images)

of the 16th century was designed with padded or brigandined wings projecting over the end of the shoulder, often en suite with a low standing collar emerging from between the shoulder straps, the sode were often discarded as superfluous.

Sode, like the kusazuri, could be of a different style from the rest of the armour. The sode and kusazuri themselves seem to have been made in matching sets.

Of all the tosei gusoku, none is more representative than the *okegawa-do*. The latter was a logical development following centuries of increased simplification. Armour had changed from thousands of lacquered scales laced together into boards that were then laced, one suspended from the other, to solid plate lames with full suspensory lacing, to solid plate lames with sparse lacing, and finally to solid plate lames riveted together.

The popularity of okegawa-do was due to a number of reasons. Firstly they were cheap and could be produced quickly. The second reason was protection. With the advent of the firearm, shot-proof armour was necessary. This cuirass was sufficiently tough. There are many examples in museums that have holes in them; whether the armour stopped the bullet or not is unknown. At the end of one battle, Tokugawa Ieyasu removed his armour only to have a handful of bullets fall out. They had pierced the metal, but it had absorbed so much of the force that he was completely unhurt and had not even noticed.

One of the most important reasons for the popularity of the okegawa-do was its versatility. Most samurai were highly individualistic and wanted their armour to reflect this. Getting noticed was a vital part of gaining advancement and promotion. Pictures in lacquer, heraldic emblems, unusual colours or patterns, domed rivets, rivets with decorative 'washers' behind them, scalloped or wavy-topped plates, the occasional laced breast board – all were methods used by armourers to 'customise' armour.

The original pattern used for kusazuri on tachi-do tosei gusoku would seem to have been designed to mirror the lames of the torso; the same number of lames would be used in the kusazuri, and the circumference at the waist would match that of the top of the kusazuri, and the circumference below the armpits would be the same as the bottom of the kusazuri. This pattern did not survive, however, and widths did vary. Kusazuri were generally wider at the bottom than at the top in all but the cheapest of suits, and in most cases the sets of tassets overlapped each other slightly.

The kusazuri seem to have been designed independently of the cuirass; the do may have been of solid plate lame construction, the kusazuri could be of scale or mock

OPPOSITE Made for the Niwa family, this armour is a *mogami-do*, laced in the *sugake-odoshi* (spaced-out-braid) style. Because of its construction from iron scales laced together, Japanese armour could progressively absorb a blow, just like a modern flak jacket, and unlike a European suit of armour.

scale (*kiritsuke kozane*). They could also be of different colours; e.g. gold kusazuri suspended from a black do. The kusazuri might be fully laced, while the do had only limited lace. Most of the time the kusazuri matched the cuirass perfectly, but there were exceptions.

By the end of the 16th century, kusazuri were increasingly suspended not from the do itself, but from a narrow belt-like strip of leather that was attached to the do. This leather 'belt' was attached to the bottom of the do either with small cords or frogs. Removable kusazuri had the advantage of making the armour easier to pack, but had few other benefits. When fording rivers, they could be removed and kept clean, dry and out of the way, but some samurai tied their kusazuri up with cord when doing this anyway, so the benefits were minor.

HELMETS

The kabuto (helmet) is one of the most readily identifiable pieces of armour the samurai wore. Warriors liked to stand out from the crowd, and the application of crests to otherwise uniform or standardised helmets was the easiest way to achieve this end.

The vast majority of helmets were of the multiplate variety, where between 8 and 32 curved, wedge-shaped plates were riveted together to form the helmet bowl. The earliest kabuto worn with o-yoroi generally were made up of only a few plates, 10 to 12 being common. (In contrast, by the time of the Sengoku Jidai, helmets of 32, 62 and 72 plates were not uncommon.)

At the crown of the kabuto, where all the plates came together, was a hole with an ornamented rim of gilt copper, called the *tehen*. Its purpose is unclear, but it was

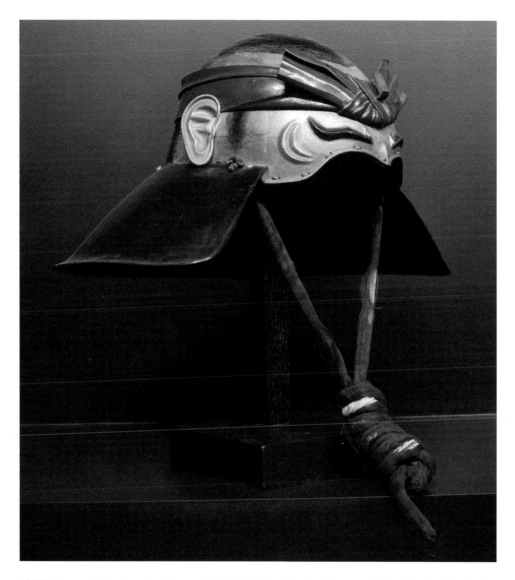

ABOVE A *zu nari* kabuto in the Ann and Gabriel Barbier-Mueller Museum, Dallas (Texas), dated to the end of the Edo Period. The photograph was taken during an exhibition in the Musée des Arts Premiers in Paris. (User: Vassil/Wikimedia Commons/CC0-1.0)

variously believed to allow the spirit of the war god Hachiman to enter the warrior, to allow the warrior to breathe under water, to allow him to sink if he should need to jump into a river and several other equally implausible possibilities. The most likely reason seems to be that at the juncture of many pointed plates of metal, cutting out the central section would be easier than joining them or overlapping them.

The first and most common multiplate helmets were simple hemispheres, or slightly tapered into an egg shape to fit the head better. A later development was the *zu nari*, or head-shaped helmet bowl, similar in shape to modern military helmets.

Hanging from the rim of the kabuto's bowl was the shikoro, the lamellar nape guard. There were many forms, but the standard was a series of concentric plates suspended one from the other. With the helmet lying on a flat surface, the lames would all telegraph up.

Between AD 700 and 1500, shikoro had three to five lames. The topmost, or sometimes the top two, had an elongated section turned back over the shikoro. Called *fukigaeshi*, they were originally intended to prevent the downward stroke of a sword from passing between lames and severing the lacing.

Shikoro were designed – pattern, lacquer and lacing – to match with the sode and kusazuri. Gold-tone shikoro hanging from a black or red lacquered bowl were not uncommon.

Some warriors (Tokugawa Ieyasu being one) had helmets with the usual lame shikoro, and hanging from the inside, a set of mail-faced cloth panels for extra protection. These were called *shita-jikoro*, or under-shikoro; the Iwai school is said to have especially favoured them.

LEFT This elaborately decorated kabuto dates from around 1560, and forms part of a suit of armour presented to Magdalen College, Oxford by Prince Chichibu. (Photo by Photo12/UIG via Getty Images)

The face – one of the most sensitive parts of the body – was usually left unprotected. Varieties of *men yoroi* (face armour) were occasionally worn; these usually took the form of a half-mask – covering the nose, cheeks and chin – of metal or leather sculptured into an angry grimace. This was the menpo. The nose was nearly always made to be removable, and indeed was more comfortable this way. Noseless varieties – called *hoate* or *hanbo* – were also very common. Full face masks (*so men*) were not very highly thought of, for, while providing protection, they restricted breathing and vision; thus they were hardly ever used.

For the early samurai the wearing of crests was a prerogative of rank, but by the 1550s, crests were common. These crests, or *datemono*, were attached to fittings on the visor, or sometimes mounted on either side of the helmet bowl. They took the form of dragonflies, butterflies, large crescent moons, horns, discs bearing heraldic emblems, and the like. The material was primarily wood and papier mâché with the details painted on.

As an alternative to crests, some had conventional helmets with decorative details such as an extravagant application of decorative rivets, or two-tone lacquer patterns. Unusual helmet designs were also common, and the variety produced during the last half of the 16th century was huge.

The *kawari kabuto*, or 'changed helmets', were restricted for practical reasons to those who could afford them (or loot them from the dead after a battle). Kawari kabuto ran the gamut from simply unusual shapes such as the peach-shaped *momo-nari* and the acorn-shaped *shii-nari*, to elaborate sculptures constructed of papier mâché and lacquer on a wood frame attached to a simple helmet bowl. Sculptures included animal heads, grimacing sea monsters, evil-looking deities' faces and tall shapes evocative of the samurai court caps.

OTHER ARMOUR

For arm protection, kote were worn from the earliest days, but the forms changed greatly. During the Heian Period modern-style kote first appeared. They resembled bags and were more useful for tucking the huge sleeves of the armour robe out of the way of the bowstring than as a defence; indeed, plates were apparently attached to it only as an afterthought.

It was not until the Gempei War, when hand-to-hand combat began to occur with regularity, that wearing a pair became common. The most common style comprised the various splint kote. The number of splints on the forearm ranged from three (broad, sometimes, but not necessarily, overlapping) to more than 20 (narrow and overlapping). The material of the sleeve itself had many layers of cloth. To this foundation were stitched the metal (or rarely leather) plates and mail.

Suneate, or greaves, usually matched the kote. Two long cords, one at the ankle and one below the knee, secured the suneate in place, both cords wrapped around the leg once and tied at the front. The inside ankle area was usually covered with or replaced by a leather panel, regardless of whether the suneate was of large plates or splints. This panel was designed to protect the stirrup strap from abrasion by the metal plates.

Though the kusazuri protected the hips and upper thighs, samurai fighting on foot needed protection for the thighs; the haidate, or 'thigh-shields', which appeared at the end of the Kamakura shogunate, served this purpose. Haidate were usually made from horizontal rows of small plates that overlapped and were loosely laced together.

'THE WAY OF THE SAMURAI IS FOUND IN DEATH'

Although every aspect of a samurai's life is important in understanding the totality of the world of the warrior, nothing is more fundamental than a knowledge of the beliefs and traditions that surround the moment the warrior took leave of the physical world. Whether that passing was voluntary or involuntary, the intense focus on the end of a samurai's life in so much of the relevant literature makes one very inclined to agree with the 17th-century samurai Yamamoto Tsunetomo, who wrote in *Hagakure* that 'the way of the samurai is found in death'.

Yet it is the handful of passages referring directly to death that have given *Hagakure* its chilling reputation. There is a long passage almost at the end of the work that reads:

LEFT Akashi Gidayu preparing to carry out *seppuku* (ritual suicide) after losing a battle for his master in 1582. He had just written his death poem and contemplates it as here with his knife readied. By Tsukioka Yoshitoshi around 1890. (Library of Congress, Washington)

Meditation on inevitable death should be performed daily. Every day when one's body and mind are at peace, one should meditate upon being ripped apart by arrows, muskets, spears and swords, being carried away by surging waves, being thrown into the midst of a great fire, being struck by lightning, being shaken to death by a great earthquake, falling from thousand-foot cliffs, dying of disease or committing *seppuku* at the death of one's master. And every day without fail one should consider oneself as dead.

Leaving aside the references to natural disasters (and earthquakes have always been a common preoccupation in Japan), because a samurai's function in life was to fight, a calm acceptance of being 'ripped apart' might almost be regarded as the warrior's stock in trade. Nor does it set the samurai apart from any other contemporary professional fighter. The phrase that makes the samurai unique is the one about committing seppuku (ritual suicide) at the death of one's master. In a handful of words we are told all we need to know about the ultimate demands that might be made on the life of the samurai. The first, seppuku, refers to the deed itself. The second, 'at the death of one's master', refers to a particular (and very controversial) set of circumstances in which the samurai might be required to perform it.

RITUAL SUICIDE

Seppuku is the correct expression for an act of suicide performed by the process of cutting open the abdomen. It is better known in the West as *hara kiri* (belly-cutting). Seppuku was commonly performed using a dagger. It could take place with preparation and ritual in the privacy of one's home, or speedily in a quiet corner of a battlefield while one's comrades kept the enemy at bay.

ABOVE The dying warrior. A mortally wounded samurai tries to rise to his feet using his bloodstained sword.

In the world of the samurai, seppuku was a deed of bravery that was admirable in a warrior who knew he was defeated, disgraced or mortally wounded. It meant that he could end his days with his transgressions wiped away and with his reputation not merely intact but actually enhanced. The cutting of the abdomen released the samurai's spirit in the most dramatic fashion, but it was an extremely painful and unpleasant way to die, and sometimes the samurai who was performing the act asked a loyal comrade to cut off his head at the moment of agony.

The earliest reference to seppuku occurs in *Hogen Monogatari*, which deals with the conflicts in which the Taira and the Minamoto were involved in 1156. The mention of the fact that a samurai called Uno Chikaharu and his followers were captured so quickly that 'they did not have time to draw their swords or cut their bellies' is so matter-of-fact that it implies that the practice was already commonplace, at least among the warriors from eastern Japan.

The first named individual to commit seppuku in the war chronicles was the celebrated archer Minamoto Tametomo, who committed suicide in this way as boatloads of Taira samurai approached his island of exile. The first recorded account of seppuku after certain defeat in a battle that was still going on is that of Minamoto Yorimasa in the first battle of Uji in 1180. His suicide was undertaken with such finesse that it was to provide a model for noble and heroic hara kiri for centuries to come.

While his sons held off the enemy, Yorimasa retired to write a poem on the back of his war fan, which read:

LEFT The suicide of Yodogimi, Toyotomi Hideyoshi's widow and the mother of Hideyori. She was very influential in accepting the peace agreement that ended Tokugawa Ieyasu's Winter campaign against Osaka Castle in 1614.

Like a fossil tree
From which we gather no flowers
Sad has been my life
Fated no fruit to produce.

Minamoto Yorimasa's sequence of poem and suicide was followed many times in later history. After the battle of Yamazaki in 1582 Akechi Mitsutoshi performed the unprecedented act of committing seppuku and writing a poem on the door with the blood from his abdomen, using a brush. Minamoto Yorimasa's classic act of seppuku was performed without the aid of a *kaishaku*, or second, to deliver a merciful blow on to his neck at the moment of agony. This was a practice that became more frequent, and much more acceptable, as the years went by, but it was never a popular duty, as Yamamoto Tsunetomo tells us:

> From ages past it has been considered ill-omened by samurai to be requested as kaishaku. The reason for this is that one gains no fame even if the job is well done. And if by chance one should blunder, it becomes a lifetime disgrace.

As a description in the *Heike Monogatari* of the defeated Taira soldiers' mass suicide by drowning in the sea battle of Dannoura shows, seppuku was not the only way of ending a samurai's life, and may have been a tradition espoused only by eastern Japanese samurai until after the time of the Gempei War. No member of the Taira family is recorded as having committed seppuku. In other cases of alternative suicide the choice of how to end one's life was dictated by circumstances. When Imai Kanehira committed suicide at the battle of Awazu in 1184, he was surrounded by enemies, so he killed himself quickly by jumping head first from his horse with his sword in his mouth.

As previously noted, at the battle of Dannoura we are told of the imperial grandmother throwing herself into the sea with the child emperor in her arms. There are many instances of samurai women committing suicide by throwing themselves from the walls of castles about to be sacked, or other cases of drowning. When done with a weapon, acts of suicide by women were likely to be performed using a dagger to the throat, and when it came to offensive weapons the traditional female costume allowed many possibilities for concealing weapons such as small narrow-bladed knives. Inazu Nitobe, using the colourful language typical of his *Bushido: The Soul of Japan*, describes their use:

> Girls, when they reached womanhood, were presented with dirks [*kaiken*, pocket poniards] which might be directed to the bosom of their assailants, or, if advisable, to their own … Her own weapon was always in her bosom. It was a disgrace for her not to know the proper way in which she had to perpetrate self-destruction.

ATONEMENT

There are several instances in samurai history of suicide being performed as a result of personal failure. Here the samurai would commit *sokotsu-shi*, or 'expiatory suicide', the very act itself wiping the slate clean. Some later examples are quite bizarre.

Legend tells us that Togo Shigechika had failed to capture a certain castle, so had himself buried alive, fully armoured and mounted on his horse, staring in the direction of his failure. Other decisions to act in this way could be spontaneous

信長記

ABOVE The suicide of Takeda Katsuyori. A section from the painted scroll in the Nagashino Castle Museum shows Takeda Katsuyori committing hara kiri as Oda Nobunaga's troops approach. Note how he has stripped off his body armour to allow himself to perform the deed unrestricted. The artist has depicted in a very graphic manner the moment when the abdomen is opened.

and dramatic, such as the action of the veteran warrior Yamamoto Kansuke at the fourth battle of Kawanakajima in 1561. As Takeda Shingen's chief strategist he had devised the plan by which the Takeda were to surprise the Uesugi army. When his bold plan apparently failed, Kansuke took his spear and plunged into the midst of the enemy army, committing suicide to make amends for his error. The tragedy of his death was that his conclusion about the destruction of the Takeda proved incorrect. Reinforcements arrived, the army rallied and a defeat was turned into victory. Yet an experienced general had been lost, one who would have served Shingen better by staying alive.

Committing suicide was not always a voluntary activity. It could be allowed as an honourable alternative to execution for a condemned criminal of the samurai class. Sasa Narimasa was 'invited' to commit suicide by Toyotomi Hideyoshi in 1588 following his disastrous handling of the territory Hideyoshi had given him.

Sometimes a daimyo was called upon to perform seppuku as the basis of a peace agreement. This would so weaken the defeated clan that resistance would effectively cease. Toyotomi Hideyoshi used an enemy's suicide in this way on several occasions, of which the most dramatic, in that it effectively ended a dynasty of daimyo forever, is what happened when the Hojo were defeated at Odawara in 1590. Hideyoshi insisted on the suicide of the retired daimyo Hojo Ujimasa, and the exile of his son Ujinao. With one sweep of a sword the most powerful daimyo family in eastern Japan disappeared from history.

Instead of the daimyo's death, the victor might be satisfied with the death of his enemy's retainer if the subordinate was in charge of the castle the victor was besieging. The most theatrical example of this occurred when Toyotomi Hideyoshi besieged Takamatsu Castle in 1582. It was a long siege, and only looked like being

successful when Hideyoshi diverted a river to make a lake that gradually began to flood the castle. Hideyoshi drew up peace terms with Mori Terumoto that included the clause that the valiant defender of Takamatsu, Shimizu Muneharu, should commit suicide. Shimizu Muneharu was determined to go to his death as dramatically as he had lived, and took a boat out into the middle of the artificial lake. When he was satisfied that Hideyoshi's men were taking careful note of what he was doing, he committed seppuku.

ABOVE A print by Yoshitoshi showing the flooding of Takamatsu Castle. (www.lacma.org)

In 1581 Tottori Castle in Inaba Province held out for an incredible 200 days before it surrendered to Hideyoshi. Its commander, Kikkawa Tsuneie, inspired his men to this long resistance even though they were reduced to eating grass and dead horses, and may even have practised cannibalism. Tsuneie's suicide was one of the conditions of surrender. His letter to his son survives to this day:

> We have endured for over 200 days. We now have no provisions left. It is my belief that by giving up my life I will help my garrison. There is nothing greater than the honour of our family. I wish our soldiers to hear of the circumstances of my death.

Another reason for committing suicide was the making of a protest. This is known as *kanshi*. Examples of this are rare, but it profoundly affected one of the greatest daimyo of the Sengoku Jidai. Oda Nobunaga inherited his father's domains at the age of 15, and although he was a brave warrior, he showed little interest in the administration of his territory. One of his best retainers, Hirade Kiyohide, tried in vain to persuade him to mend his ways, but when the young Nobunaga showed no inclination to listen to him, Kiyohide put all his feelings into a letter to his lord and committed seppuku in protest. Nobunaga was greatly moved, and changed his ways for the better, with, of course, considerable consequences for the history of Japan.

FOLLOWING IN DEATH

Junshi (following in death) is the second element in Yamamoto Tsunetomo's exhortation to preparedness for death in *Hagakure*, when he insists on a willingness to perform seppuku on the death of one's master. Again there are early examples to be found in the war chronicles. In *Hogen Monogatari*, when Minamoto Yoshitomo ordered the execution of his younger brothers, the boys' attendants killed themselves immediately afterwards. Four committed seppuku. Two others stabbed each other. *Hogen Monogatari* comments:

> Though it was their duty to have the same death, though to go forth to the place of battle to be struck down with one's lord and to cut one's belly is the usual custom, on the grounds that there had not yet been such an example as this, there was no one who did not praise it.

When Kamakura was captured in 1333, we read of many acts of suicide, including this classic account of junshi:

> The retainers who were left behind ran out to the middle gate, crying aloud, 'Our lord has killed himself. Let all loyal men accompany him!' Then these 20 lit a fire in the mansion, quickly lined up together in the smoke and cut their bellies. And not willing to be outdone, 300 other warriors cut their bellies and leapt into the consuming flames.

There are examples of junshi being performed even before the daimyo was dead. Shortly before Shimizu Muneharu's dramatic suicide on the artificial lake of Takamatsu in 1582, one of his retainers invited Muneharu to his room. The loyal retainer explained that he wished to reassure his master about the ease with which

RIGHT Matsunaga Hisahide was a master of the tea ceremony, and when he was forced to commit suicide after his castle fell he began by smashing his favourite priceless tea kettle so that it would not fall into the hands of his enemies.

seppuku could be performed. He explained that he had in fact already committed suicide, and, pulling aside his robe, showed Muneharu his severed abdomen. Muneharu was touched by the gesture, and acted as his retainer's second to bring the act to a speedy and less painful conclusion by cutting off the man's head.

Although *Hogen Monogatari* commends the practice, junshi was the one reason for committing suicide that did not meet with universal approval. However inspiring the example may have been to one's fellow samurai, there were many circumstances when junshi merely added more unnecessary deaths to an existing disaster. The death of a daimyo may or may not have brought about the extinction of his house, but the practice of junshi by the senior retainers who would otherwise support and guide the lord's infant heir only made extinction more likely. A spontaneous gesture on the battlefield was understandable and even forgivable, and in the confusion of a battle the circumstances of a retainer's death could never be clearly established. But when the death of a daimyo from natural causes during times of peace provoked the performance of junshi, such an act was almost universally condemned. In such cases a loyal retainer committed suicide to show that he could serve none other than his departed lord.

During the Sengoku Jidai some retainers did have little left to live for, but in the later times of peace junshi was hardly helpful in maintaining the stability of a dynasty. In the early Edo Period as many as 20 leading retainers of various daimyo were known to have committed junshi on the deaths of their lords.

A better way to serve one's departed lord, the shogun argued, was to render equally loyal service to his heir, but junshi was firmly engrained in the Japanese mentality. A strong condemnation of it is found in the *Toshogu goikun*, the House Laws left by the first Tokugawa shogun in 1616. But at the death of his grandson the third Tokugawa shogun (Iemitsu) in 1651, five of the leading retainers of the Tokugawa committed junshi, a remarkable gesture against the law they themselves had formulated. A further attempt to ban it was introduced by the shogunate in 1663, and included the statement:

> In the event that a lord has a presentiment that a certain vassal is liable to immolate himself, he should admonish him strongly against it during his lifetime. If he fails to do so, it shall be counted as his fault. His heir will not escape appropriate punishment.

From the mid-17th century onwards the practice of junshi effectively ceased until it came dramatically to the attention of modern Japan in 1912. On the eve of the funeral of Emperor Meiji, General Nogi Maresuke and his wife committed suicide. Nogi had commanded troops in the Sino-Japanese War of 1894–95, and led the battle to take Port Arthur in the Russo-Japanese War of 1904–05. It was an act that astounded his contemporaries because of the bizarre disloyalty to the emperor's wishes that the illegal act implied. It was also sobering evidence that the samurai spirit lived on in the Japan of the 20th century.

THE 47 RONIN

The famous 47 Ronin were loyal samurai retainers of Asano Naganori (1667–1701), who was based in the town of Ako in Harima Province. In 1700 Naganori, together with a certain Kira Yoshihisa, was commissioned to entertain envoys of the emperor at the court of the shogun. Kira Yoshihisa held the office of Master of Ceremonies, and it was the custom that his colleague should give him some presents in order to get instruction from him and thus avoid any error of etiquette. When Asano Naganori brought no gifts, Yoshihisa – deeply offended – wasted no opportunity to scorn his colleague. One day Naganori lost his temper, drew his short sword and wounded Yoshihisa on the forehead. Even to draw a weapon in the presence of the shogun was a very serious matter, so Naganori was arrested. He was ordered to commit seppuku, and carried out the act the same day that he had attacked Yoshihisa.

The shogun added to the agony by deciding that the territory of Ako should be confiscated as punishment. By this act Asano Naganori's retainers were to be made unemployed and dispossessed. They would become ronin (masterless samurai, literally 'men of the waves'), and it was at this point that they decided to avenge their dead lord. The chief retainer Oishi Yoshio

Kuranosuke retired to Kyoto, where he began to plot a secret revenge with the 46 others. Kira Yoshihisa suspected a plot against him, but his spies only found men apparently addicted to drink and given to pleasure.

On a snowy night in December 1702, Naganori's retainers took sudden revenge on Yoshihisa at his mansion in Edo. The guards were taken by surprise, the doors broken in with huge mallets, and a fierce swordfight ensued. Kuranosuke cut off Yoshihisa's head and placed it on Naganori's tomb in the Sengakuji temple in recognition that a solemn duty had been fulfilled. They also left a written address to their dead lord:

We, who have eaten of your food, could not without blushing repeat the verse, 'Thou shalt not live under the same heaven nor tread the same earth with the enemy of your father or lord,' nor could we have dared to leave hell and present ourselves before you in paradise, unless we had carried out the vengeance which you began.

One of the ronin had been killed in the raid, so it was the remaining 46 who went to the authorities and proclaimed what they had done. This placed the government in a quandary. The samurai of Ako had fulfilled their moral

近松勘六源行重
三十四歳

大髙源五源忠雄
三十二歳

Four of the celebrated 47 Ronin, whose revenge killing stunned contemporary Japan. This scroll is in the Oish
Shrine in Banshu-Ako.

duty but had broken the law, and, theoretically at least in the Neo-Confucian world of Tokugawa Japan, law and moral duty could not come into conflict.

Even in a society that valued the notion of revenge, a man was not entirely free to do as he liked, and during the 17th century a system had emerged of registered vendetta, called *kataki uchi*. However, this did not allow for avenging the death of one's lord, only a relative, and as the vengeance of the Ako samurai depended on surprise, registration would have been impossible anyway.

The decision the government reached was that

the law must be upheld at all costs, so the ronin were ordered to commit seppuku – a course of action for which they had been prepared from the start. Although the reaction from their contemporaries was not so enthusiastic, later generations came to idolise the 47 Ronin. One commentator wrote: 'from scholars ministers and gentlemen down to cart pullers and grooms, there is no one who does not slap his thighs in admiration.' Officially criminals, they could still be worshipped as *chushin gishi* (loyal and dutiful samurai who sacrificed their lives for a transcendent cause

THE SAMURAI AT WAR

THE CALL TO ARMS

When a call to arms took place, the samurai such as the daimyo's elite guards who inhabited the castle complex were immediately transferred from guard duty to campaign duty. For others some form of muster had to be carried out, and various documents survive to show how daimyo converted their part-time samurai into full-time fighters. The process depended on the degree of professionalism within a daimyo's system and the closeness of the ties between him and the vassals being summoned.

An interesting example is provided by the samurai of Chosokabe Motochika (1539–99), who conquered the whole of Shikoku island using samurai who were also farmers. They would tend their rice fields up to their knees in mud but with the boxes containing their precious suits of armour lying on the paths between the paddy fields and their spears thrust into the ground with their straw sandals dangling from them. When the alarm sounded, they downed tools and became samurai once again. These 'minutemen' were sufficient when all that Motochika had to face were similarly equipped samurai in neighbouring provinces, but they proved to be no match for Toyotomi Hideyoshi when he invaded Shikoku in 1585.

LEFT Detail from a painted screen of the 12th-century Gempei War. Tosa School, Edo Period. (Photo by DeAgostini/Getty Images)

Hideyoshi's own mobilisation was a far more complex affair. He could call on his own virtually professional samurai, but as his conquests proceeded, he was also able to summon the daimyo who had accepted vassal status to serve under him. The preparations for the invasion of Korea in 1592 provide some excellent examples. Goto Sumiharu, who held the fief of Fukue on the Goto Islands, had an assessed income of 140,000 koku, which by the sliding scale in operation required him to supply 840 men for the Korean campaign. He actually provided only 705, broken down as shown in the following table:

Goto Sumiharu in person	1
Bugyo (army commissioners)	5
Messengers	3
Inspectors	2
Mounted samurai	11
Foot samurai	40
Samurai's armed attendants	38
Ashigaru	120
Priests, doctors, secretaries	5
Labourers	280
Boatmen	200
Total	705

The figures therefore include 220 fighting men but more than double that number of non-combatants who acted in a supportive function.

ON THE MARCH

When an army was ready to march off, the samurai would be inspected and would watch and wait as their leader performed a number of rituals of departure. The most important act was to pray for victory. Certain Buddhist deities were particularly favoured as bringers of victory and destroyers of evil. One's enemies were of course evil by definition, so powerful gods like Fudo 'the immoveable one' would be enlisted to smite them. Buddhist priests would offer up such prayers on a daimyo's behalf either by chanting or writing prayers on wooden sticks called *goma* which were ceremonially burned. Just before the fifth battle of Kawanakajima in 1564 Uesugi Kenshin offered up a prayer for victory at a nearby Hachiman shrine. The text, which has been preserved, consists largely of a catalogue of his enemy Takeda Shingen's misdeeds, beginning with the forced exile of his father. Kenshin lists seven categories of Shingen's wrongdoing including several failures of a religious nature. Shingen, he states, had been remiss in overseeing religious ceremonies and had assigned secular authorities to supervise temples and shrines when he invaded Shinano. The prayers then posed a question and a challenge to Hachiman:

> Now that Shingen has destroyed Shinano's temples and shrines and exiled their priests, who could possibly respect the authority of the kami if they allow him to continue gaining victories?

The traditional farewell meal of *kachi guri* ('victory' chestnuts), *kombu* (kelp) and awabi (abalone) washed down with sake was the last ritual of departure before the daimyo took his signalling fan and shouted '*Ei! Ei!*' to which the samurai replied '*Oh!*'. As an example we may take the grand departure from Sosaengp'o Castle in 1598 of Japan's great hero general Kato Kiyomasa:

Kiyomasa put on his black laced armour, tightened the cords of his helmet … and taking along 15 pages, 15 messengers, 20 guns and 35 foot soldiers, jumped into a small boat, set up his standard and shouted '*Ei! Ei!*'

An army on the march was a spectacular sight. The best-known images of thousands of samurai marching by come from woodblock prints of the Edo Period, where martial processions were required of the daimyo. We see them armed to the teeth on their way to pay their respects to the shogun, with flags flying and spears shouldered. A march to war a few decades earlier cannot have looked much different, and was attended by very strict discipline. Tokugawa Ieyasu's orders for behaviour during the advance to Odawara in 1590 run to 12 articles and include admonitions about marching order and prohibitions against letting horses stray loose in camp. The document ends with a warning that the 'gods and Buddhas will blast transgressors', but Ieyasu's own officers did quite a bit of blasting themselves. Gamo Ujisato noted that one samurai with a rather distinctive helmet was not keeping his place and ordered him to do so. On a further turn of inspection the man was out of place again, so Ujisato calmly drew his sword and lopped off the man's head. He gave the splendid helmet to someone else.

Given Japan's rough, mountainous terrain, and the lack of such things as baggage wagons, campaigns and maintaining lines of supply while in the field were rather more difficult than elsewhere.

COMMUNICATIONS

There was more to achieving victory on a Sengoku Jidai battlefield than sending one's samurai spearmen forward in an impetuous charge against a line of foot soldiers or

ABOVE The most important of audible communications devices were the drum, conch-shell trumpet and bell. The great *taiko* drums could be used for setting a marching pace, and there were complex trumpet calls used for signalling. Here Toyotomi Hideyoshi is shown sounding a conch shell.

a castle wall. Good logistics were needed, and these were underpinned by robust communications systems within a daimyo's province, and equally efficient ones on the micro level of the battlefield.

The most important strategic communications function was that of rapidly transmitting throughout one's territory the knowledge of any threatening movement by a neighbour. Takeda Shingen, for example, established a complex network of fire beacons across Kai Province, so that any move by his great rival Uesugi Kenshin could be notified to his capital at Kofu as quickly as possible.

The beacons were maintained in wooden towers. Combustible material kept ready in a bucket was lit and swung up into the air on a long pivoting arm. Once the nature and severity of the threat had been assessed, a call to arms could begin among the part-time soldiers and farmers through the communication medium of a runner, a bell or a conch-shell trumpet. The troops would then report to the nearest castle.

When a samurai army was on the march, scouts would be sent on ahead to report back on enemy movements. Sometimes a scouting operation would take the form of a 'reconnaissance in force', with the unit deliberately coming to grips with the enemy ranks to test their mettle. The men chosen for this vital task were always both excellent horsemen and brave fighters, and their exploits are celebrated in chronicles such as *Hojo Godaiki*, where the bravery of the horses is also commended in one incident when two Hojo scouts were surrounded and almost captured.

Messages from the scouts would be delivered to the daimyo at great personal risk to the messenger, and could be either verbal or written. A good example of verbal communications from scouts is the battle of Chiksan in Korea in 1597. Here the advance guard came upon a large Chinese army and sent scouts back to the main body while the rest of the force engaged the enemy to buy time; in fact the sound of firing transferred the gist of their message much more quickly than did the galloping horsemen. It is also interesting to note that many surviving letters containing official information end with the words: 'You will be informed of these things by the messenger.' This was in case the written message was intercepted by the enemy.

During sieges, written messages were delivered over the walls of a castle by the time-honoured method of the arrow letter, a device noted frequently during the siege of Hara Castle in 1638, although signalling arrows existed that had a hollow, turnip-shaped wooden head and whistled as they flew through the air. These were traditionally used at the start of a battle and were regarded as a call to the gods to witness the brave deeds that were about to take place. During the 12th century signal arrows began the archery duel between mounted samurai bowmen, but by the Sengoku Jidai this procedure had long since been replaced by hundreds of ashigaru firing a volley of arquebus bullets.

The messengers on a battlefield were drawn from the same elite samurai ranks as the scouts but had the more restricted role of communication between friendly troops rather than intelligence gathering. They had to be very easily recognised in the heat and smoke of battle, so were often distinguished by their horo cloaks.

BATTLEFIELD MEDICINE

Any wounded had to be treated in the field: there was no way to evacuate them behind the lines. After the battle, the best a seriously wounded man could hope for – after a little bit of medical attention – was to be retired from the campaign to a temple or house where he could possibly recuperate. Those with minor wounds had to recover in the field with their comrades. A seriously wounded samurai, however, would be likely

ABOVE The most feared arrow wound was one in the face or throat, not only for the potentially fatal outcome, but for the painful 'treatment'. The warrior's head was secured to a tree to keep him still, and the arrow was removed by a physician (or a comrade, if none was available) who would resort to pliers if the arrowhead was barbed. (Angus McBride © Osprey Publishing)

to die on the battlefield because medical treatment was either primitive or unavailable, although doctors do appear on the muster lists for some campaigns. The cuts produced by samurai swords must have led to hundreds of warriors simply bleeding to death. Minor cuts could, however, by treated by applying *yomogi* (mugwort), a known coagulant. Acupuncture was also available. A medical manual of the 14th century quoted by Thomas Conlan includes the following recommendation for dealing with abdominal wounds: 'Cover the intestines with dried faeces, then close the wound with mulberry root sutures and spread cat-tail pollen over the area.' Activities to be avoided were 'anger, laughter, thought, sex, activity, work, sour foods and sake'. Somehow one imagines that a recuperating samurai might not have much trouble avoiding laughter, but it is interesting to note the use of horse faeces two centuries later. According to *Hagakure*, Amari Tozo of the Takeda army was faced with a samurai who had received a deep wound and whose blood would not clot. Tozo ordered him to drink the faeces of a red-haired horse mixed with water. The man was most reluctant to take his medicine until Tozo set the useful example of drinking some first.

In addition, armies on the march would stop at hot springs and natural spas whenever possible, especially after an engagement, to partake of the waters in the belief that they could help alleviate various ailments. Takeda Shingen was famous for being a proponent of the health-restoring waters, and his domains are peppered with sites of spas at which he supposedly stayed.

FOOD

Rice was the staple of the soldier on campaign just as it was for those at home. While his meals were simple, he tried to supplement the diet with whatever was available;

if there was a stream nearby, he tried to catch some fish, or perhaps he would make a soup from fish-stock (usually instant, made with stored dried bonito shavings) and whatever leaves and vegetables he could find. Invariably there was a supply of pickled vegetables that had been brought along in the baggage train.

Warriors considered pork, boar and rabbit to be 'stamina' foods, useful to help them keep their energy up. Although most were at least nominally Buddhist (and therefore in theory vegetarians), the restriction against eating the meat of living creatures was broken regularly with little soul-searching.

The samurai carried their own version of instant food and 'iron rations' on campaign. This common food was rice that had been pre-cooked and allowed to dry. This product, similar to today's minute rice (though slightly more cooked to start with), was carried in pouches ready to eat – crunchy and incredibly dry, but filling – or mixed with a very small amount of water and boiled to make instant rice.

Cooking gear was also carried, but many samurai of the lower ranks seem to have done their cooking inside their upturned helmets. Like modern military units, a group of samurai may have taken turns running mess duties at breakfast, lunch, dinner and so on.

CAMPS

Samurai had to make do with whatever shelter they could make or find. The generals and lords commandeered temples to billet themselves and their staff, while their guards, servants and the common soldiery slept in surrounding buildings, stables, under trees, in farmhouses or in the open air.

Tents and pavilions do not seem to have played a major part in the campaigns of Japan. This is probably due to the difficulty in transporting such bulky items and

the fact that there were temples and shrines in abundance ready made to provide more than adequate shelter.

A *honjin*, or main camp, was always erected as the command centre. It was usually ringed by crested camp curtains (*jinmaku*, or *tobari*). The films *Kagemusha* and *Ran* show such camps accurately. From here, surrounded by guards, the general oversaw the battle.

ABOVE Seated within his maku with his hatamoto, Tokugawa Ieyasu directs the battle of Sekigahara, 1600, in this detail from a painted screen in the Watanabe Collection, Tottori. When setting out on a long-planned campaign an army might augment the maku into a more solid temporary defence like a Roman castrum, with fences and ditches.

FIELD REPAIRS

To cut down on baggage, armour was worn almost constantly. Long summer campaigns quickly proved uncomfortable, and armour became host to lice and other vermin. To alleviate this, armour was sometimes suspended over wet fires and 'smoked'.

With all the wear and tear on the armour (be it from damage on the battlefield or through weeks of exposure to the elements), samurai often found what little spare time they had occupied with maintenance and minor repairs. These repairs were done in the field by the warrior himself; armourers never accompanied the armies.

Stringing a few cords through lames that had had their lacing severed was a simple repair. It was also easy to patch the foundation cloth of the armoured sleeves, greaves or thigh protection. Anything beyond that would likely require a specialist, as lacquer would need to be removed and reapplied in addition to whatever work might be required on the plate itself.

When armour was damaged beyond what these simple field repairs could fix, lower-class warriors often just scrapped the piece and picked up a replacement. It was usually simple to acquire such items on campaign by looting from the enemy or stripping the dead. Upper-class samurai were expected to have it repaired or even buy replacements, rather than resorting to scavenging among the corpses on the field.

OPPOSITE This samurai, a retainer of the Honda family, is dressed in the tosei gusoku (modern armour) that became universal towards the end of the Period of Warring States. His helmet, the only trace of flamboyance in his otherwise sombre costume, is a momonari kabuto (peach-shaped helmet). His weapon of choice is an arquebus, unusual perhaps for a samurai, but as he would have a man to keep him reloaded and supplied it was a perfectly practical proposition. About his person he carries a bamboo canteen, a powder flask and bullet pouch, a sleeping mat and ration bags. (Angus McBride © Osprey Publishing)

To that end, many clans had specialists in giving battered armour a second life, and after a campaign, these craftsmen were kept very busy.

THE BURDEN OF THE WARRIOR

Due to the mountainous nature of the Japanese archipelago, pack wagons, carts and wheeled vehicles in general were virtually non-existent outside the cities. As a result, the task of hauling supplies and equipment fell upon large numbers of packhorses and the samurai themselves. A warrior going on campaign was loaded down with more than his weapons. He generally carried his own food, clothing, gear and medicines, in addition to being a human packhorse for the army's supplies.

Rations were carried to the field by each samurai in a long, narrow sack. A meal's worth of cooked rice in the form of *onigiri* (riceballs) or a day's worth of raw rice (sources conflict, but it is likely that both methods were used, depending on the campaign, although the same amount of raw rice would go farther) was placed in the sack, and then tied off. The next ration followed, and

In 1274 a Mongol armada from China, 800 ships and 30,000 men strong, arrived off the Japanese coast. The first islands on the way to Kyushu were soon overrun. The defenders were shocked at the foreign style of fighting: warfare in Japan was highly ritualised and purely an affair between *bushi* (warriors), but the Mongols and their Korean conscripts conducted wholesale massacres. Samurai were trained in individual combat, men of similar rank calling out challenges and engaging each other, whereas the invaders fought in huge massed formations with wholly different tactics. Frantic requests for help were sent to Kamakura.

The Mongols soon reached Kyushu and forced the defenders to entrench. They were surprised at the desperate strength of the resistance; and, having used up much of their provisions and materiel in what they had expected to be quick shock-attacks, were in serious need of resupply. The Mongol ships were pulling out of Hakata harbour in search of a safe port (fearing night-time raids while in enemy territory) when the rains began.

Like an answer to a prayer, a huge typhoon hit the ships hard; the reinforcements requested by the bakufu never had to engage the enemy. Several thousands of Mongols died as their ships foundered, struck one another or ran aground, leaving the continental soldiers as easy pickings for the samurai on shore. The few ships that were able limped back to Korea, where records show that over 13,000 men had lost their lives during the attempted invasion.

In 1281 a second attack came, aimed at the same harbour – where the Kamakura government had built a large defensive wall in the intervening years. This attack was much larger, however: 4,000 ships and 200,000 men were involved. Fortunately for Japan, the attack was split into two parts and the over-anxious commander of the smaller, southern fleet sailed about a month early. Again, however, the attackers were amazed at the determination of the defending samurai. So fierce was the resistance that for days, even though the ships lay in the harbours, they were unable to land their troops. Disease and food shortages plagued the enemy. The Japanese were playing a desperate waiting game which they had no way of winning.

When the Mongols' large northern fleet arrived at the rendezvous, the defending samurai knew that they could not hold off engaging the enemy much longer. On 15 August the retired emperor's prayer for divine intervention was presented at the Grand Shrine

The samurai commander Suenaga Takezaki, here shown struggling to control his wounded horse, leads his forces against Mongol and Korean arrows and bombs at the battle of Torikai-gata during the first invasion. *Moko Shura Ekotoba* scroll, 1293. (Wikimedia Commons/PD-US)

of Ise to his ancestor the sun goddess Amaterasu. That evening, a miracle occurred. The skies grew dark, and the wind began to blow. Ships were dashed against the rocks, splintered and fell apart. This was the true kamikaze, the 'wind of the gods'. Once again the weather had turned the invaders away; at least

The Khan wanted to raise a third and even large assault, but probably due to resistance to the expense involved, the attack never materialised. The Great Khan was not the only one feeling financial burden of the two invasions: the Hojo government was nearly bankrupted rewarding samurai who fought, and paying for the

that was tied off. A full rations sack would have 10–15 'spheres' of rice. The remaining ends would be tied together and the sack would be worn around the shoulders.

Over his shoulders he might have carried a rolled-up straw mat. This mat would be used to cover himself as he slept, though some used it as a ground sheet. A second sack, usually worn at the waist, contained a change of clothing and whatever personal items the warrior may need; for example, something to patch his clothing with, a few yards of string for quick field repairs to his armour, fire-starting tools, writing implements, grooming aids, and the like. Just about everything else hung from his waist: canteens formed from a section of bamboo or hollowed-out gourds; pouches for medicines or dried rice; in later periods, spare matches for his matchlock firearm; spare bowstrings; and some spare *waraji* (straw sandals).

If an arquebusier, he may have carried a case of preloaded matchlock cartridges (*hayago*) on his waist sash. Spare shot was carried in a pouch at his waist as well. Samurai carried the flask for powder hanging from the toggles where the shoulderboards fastened to the cuirass. Each arquebusier also carried his own spare matches (sometimes as many as four spools, good enough for several days in the field).

If an archer, he would carry a bow (yumi), and wear a quiver (*utsubo*) at his right hip. The quiver was worn at the hip because in Japan arrows were drawn by grasping the shaft behind the arrowhead, up, out and down from the quiver. This was unlike European arrows, which were grasped by the fletched end and drawn up over the shoulder.

Samurai serving as lancers made up the backbone of the Sengoku Jidai armies. A lancer carried a long lance instead of all the equipment of an arquebusier or archer; however, in addition to the yari, he was often burdened with other gear as well. He may have been responsible for carrying on his back one of the gunpowder chests.

Each of these contained enough powder for dozens of gunners to maintain hours of continuous fire. He might carry a case of arrows intended to resupply a dozen or more archers. Other items included large drums used for signalling, a unit standard or even a portable kitchen.

If not packing a large box on his back, the samurai wore a large banner, or sashimono, bearing his lord's crest. These took several forms, including large feathered designs. Sometimes, a smaller banner would be attached to one or both sode to identify the unit to which the man was attached.

THE EXPERIENCE OF BATTLE

The night before a battle would be a lonely one for a samurai. These supposedly super warriors were only human after all, and felt fear. During the 14th century one samurai wrote to his wife and told her that he felt 'so alone' now that battle was imminent. It was a time for prayers to one's own personal choice of kami, and an opportunity to purify oneself by abstaining from sex, or by not eating venison, a meat that was regarded as ritually harmful. Alternatively a samurai could simply get drunk.

When the day of battle dawned (and dawn attacks were quite common) the samurai moved into action. If the battle was not a sneak attack, he might have been surprised to see crowds gathering to witness the spectacle. When Tachibana Muneshige assaulted Otsu Castle in 1600 on behalf of Tokugawa Ieyasu, the local townspeople turned out to watch. The slopes of Mount Hiei beside the temple of Miidera provided an excellent vantage point out of range of stray bullets, so they took along picnic boxes and settled down to enjoy the show.

When a samurai entered battle, he moved onto a stage to play the role for which his entire life and training had prepared him. Superman or coward, the samurai was about to move from theory to reality. He was surrounded by his comrades as he sat on his horse, or stood with spear in hand. His officers would have organised him, and somewhere near the spot where the largest flags were flying was his daimyo whom he had pledged to serve. Would he be thinking about the examples he had heard of his illustrious ancestors in similar situations in the past? How would he acquit himself? Would he take a head, or was this the day he died?

Perhaps the desire to be the first into the attack was uppermost in his mind. This was a potent source of samurai glory as testified by many ancestral anecdotes. Suicidal advances and even cheating were readily enlisted to win this accolade for a particular samurai. At the second battle of Uji in 1184 two samurai raced their horses across a river to be first into battle, and 400 years later the same obsession ruled.

In the press of battle the swinging of a sword was greatly restricted, and Japanese armour gave good protection, so it was rare for a man to be killed with one sweep of a sword blade unless the blow was so powerful that it would split an opponent's helmet in two. Sword fighting from a horse was not easy, because the normally two-handed katana then had to be used in one hand, but this disadvantage was somewhat overcome by the samurai's position above a foot soldier and the momentum of his horse. The process was helped by the curvature of the sword's blade, which allowed the very hard and extremely sharp cutting edge to slice into an opponent along a small area that would open up as the momentum of the swing continued to cut through to the bone. Historical records show that some samurai survived multiple cuts from sword blades. One victim was still alive after 13 strokes found their mark, and on a separate occasion a horse endured seven slashes.

The painted screens and scrolls of the period show much more use being made of spears from horseback than of swords. Ashigaru are run through, while rival horsemen are transfixed through the neck and lifted off their saddles. At the fourth battle of Kawanakajima in 1561 Takemata Hirotsuna was knocked off his horse with such force that his helmet was dislodged from his head. Other polearms were also used to great effect. At the battle of Anegawa in 1570 Makara Naotaka covered the retreat of the Asakura army by wielding a nodachi with a 5ft-long blade from horseback.

ABOVE Following the example set by Sasaki Takatsuna and Kajiwara Kagesue, hundreds of Minamoto samurai rode into the Uji River while their comrades fought across the damaged bridge.

HEAD COLLECTING

Head collecting is a tradition found throughout samurai history. For example, the chronicle *Yamamoto Toyohisa Shiki*, which refers to the Osaka campaign of 1614–15, records: 'That night 23 heads were taken. At dawn on the 17th day 24 men were summoned before Hideyori … and received rewards of gold.'

When a battle was won, the taking, recording and presentation of these ghastly trophies was as systematic and thorough as possible. In an ideal situation the heads would be viewed in a ritualised ceremony by the victorious daimyo, seated on a camp stool and surrounded by his closest retainers. He would not wish to be presented with a bloody trophy, so the heads were carefully cleaned and dressed, made presentable by cosmetics and the hair combed. They would be mounted on a spiked wooden board with labels for identification.

This routine was a task traditionally done by women, and there is a rare eyewitness account from Oan, the daughter of a samurai. She experienced the horror of sleeping beside a collection of severed heads in Ogaki Castle at the time of the battle of Sekigahara in 1600. The castle was under constant attack from the superior forces of Tokugawa Ieyasu, and her description of her work with heads is as follows:

We attached a tag to each head in order to identify them properly. Then we repeatedly blackened their teeth. Why did we do that? A long time ago, blackened teeth were admired as the sign of a distinguished man. So, we were asked to apply a generous coat of black dye to any heads with white teeth. Even these severed heads no longer held any terror for me. I used to sleep enveloped by the bloody odour of those old heads.

The correct identification of the head and the name of the samurai who had taken it was crucial. This was a change from the 12th century, when quantity had mattered more than quality. By the time of the Sengoku Jidai the samurai who decapitated an abandoned or anonymous corpse was an object of scorn, and the heads of ashigaru taken in the heat of battle might often be discarded.

If the head-viewing ceremony was to be held with no time for preparation, the heads could be presented on an opened war fan with a paper handkerchief or some leaves to soak up any dripping blood. But it was unwise to rush, and sometimes a victorious general was too ready to relax and enjoy the head inspection after his victory. On one celebrated occasion this led to a victory being turned into a defeat. Imagawa Yoshimoto was viewing heads taken from a captured fortress as he rested in a narrow wooded gorge near Okehazama in 1560. A few minutes later he was surprised by Oda Nobunaga and was himself beheaded.

There were, however, times when head collecting had to be discouraged. When Hojo Ujiyasu was preparing for the night attack that saved Kawagoe Castle in 1545, he forbade the taking of heads so that his samurai would not be distracted from their mission. A less draconian measure was to allow heads to be taken but then discarded, with rewards being subsequently granted on the basis of reliable eyewitnesses.

Head collecting also presented problems if a samurai, having taken a valuable head, abandoned the fight. This was hardly conducive to the achievement of victory. A battle could be disrupted because a samurai trying to take a head attracted several enemy samurai in an effort to stop him.

Head viewing could be delayed until a more dramatic occasion presented itself. The classic instance is the New Year's banquet thrown by Oda Nobunaga in 1574, where the coup de théâtre was the presentation by his closest retainers of the heads of Asakura Yoshikaga, Asai Hisamasa and Asai Nagamasa. All had been taken in the previous year, and each had been preserved by being lacquered and coated in gold dust.

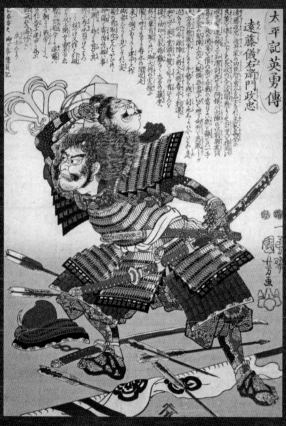

The samurai pictured is Endo Naotsugu, who tried to kill Oda Nobunaga during the battle of Anegawa in 1570. He approached Nobunaga in the guise of a friendly warrior presenting him with a severed head, and when his true purpose was discovered he threw the head in the direction of his intended victim and died fighting.

ABOVE This detail from a painted screen depicting the battle of Nagakute depicts a quite unusual event. A samurai is taking a defeated enemy prisoner and tying his hands behind his back. This would normally only happen with high-ranking enemies whom a victorious daimyo sought to humiliate by a public execution.

At the siege of Ulsan in 1598 Reizei Motomitsu spun his naginata 'like a waterwheel' to kill at least 15 Chinese soldiers.

The noise and confusion of a Sengoku Jidai battle was considerably greater than attended the clashes of the Gempei War four centuries earlier. Armies were much larger and the introduction of firearms had added greatly to the cacophony. The clouds of smoke from arquebuses would have obscured a samurai's view in a way unknown to his ancestors, and would therefore frustrate him in the samurai's other legendary pursuit of seeking a suitable opponent for single combat. The wearing of distinctive sashimono went some way to correcting the trend, however, so that at Nagashino one samurai who took the head of a Takeda follower wearing a flag sashimono with an obviously personalised design believed he had killed a victim of some importance. This was confirmed after the battle when the head was identified as being that of Mochizuki Nobumasa, the cousin of the Takeda daimyo Takeda Katsuyori. During the Korean campaign high-ranking Chinese or Korean officers stood out because of the quality of their armour and became prime targets for glory-seeking samurai.

SIEGES

Sieges were the most taxing form of warfare, both for the besieger and the besieged. Those in the fortress faced rationing as the least of their discomforts. Boredom could also undermine morale. They also faced the ever-present hazards of disease and starvation. The besiegers were under the constant threat of 'sniping' and feared possible attack by relief forces. They had less to fear from raids, however, and food was usually easier to acquire.

ABOVE From the 1560s onwards the castles of the Period of Warring States were defended by firearms as well as bows and arrows. Here we see the muzzles of arquebuses protruding from gunports in the walls of a castle in 1583. From a painted screen depicting the battle of Shizugatake in Osaka Castle Museum.

In 1582 Toyotomi Hideyoshi laid siege to Takamatsu Castle, a Mori stronghold. Rather than engaging in a protracted siege, he ordered a mile-long dam built near the low-lying castle, and then constructed dykes. When the rising waters reached the castle compound, marsh animals and vermin fled inside the walls, and the wells and supplies were flooded with brackish water. The Mori commander sued for peace, and only the assassination of Oda Nobunaga, forcing Hideyoshi to call off the siege, avoided a major defeat for the Mori.

Usually the sieges were more conventional. The Japanese never really developed effective cannon, although they had a few, and Tokugawa Ieyasu used them (mostly for psychological effect) at Sekigahara in 1600. It is due to a lack of conventional artillery that Japanese castles developed along different lines from European castles.

Samurai laying siege to a castle or other fortification would hide behind screens of wood or packed bamboo, firing at the defenders through small slots. The defenders returned fire from arrow and arquebus holes in their own fortifications. Victory for the besiegers was the result of the castle being fired, the garrison surrendering (because of disease, starvation or the like), treachery from within or storming the walls. The defenders were reliant on the arrival of a relief force or their own abilities to inflict sufficient damage on their besiegers to force them to withdraw.

The position of the defender in a siege was extremely difficult and it may be for this reason that battles were much more common. A battle might end with the losing side retreating to its nearest fortress, and this could turn into a siege. Few lords trusted to such a defence, however, preferring to take their chances in the field. In most cases (though there were exceptions), when a noble retired to his castle, he was planning to make a last stand, or at least expecting to. Shibata Katsuie and Asai Nagamasa were only two lords who perished in their keeps as the flames rose about them.

STRONGHOLDS OF THE SAMURAI

The siege and subsequent battle of Nagashino in 1575 together make up one of the pivotal events in samurai history. It began unremarkably. The army of Takeda Katsuyori had invaded Tokugawa Ieyasu's Mikawa Province, and being frustrated by their primary objective, laid siege instead to the tiny but stubbornly defended fortress of Nagashino. The siege, which lasted nearly 10 days, was a classic of the old style, conducted against a traditional castle built mainly from wood with some stone. Included in its defence were a modest number of arquebuses and only one cannon. Attacks upon it involved an assault party on a raft floated down the river, mining on the landward side, fire arrows loosed against the wooden buildings, but, above all, repeated assaults on the walls involving hand-to-hand fighting.

Oda Nobunaga, the powerful neighbouring daimyo who was destined to rise to great heights, sent an army to relieve Nagashino. When the relieving army arrived, the Takeda abandoned their siege lines to give battle. The great strength

LEFT Built in 1596 and retaining its original keep and stonework, Matsumoto Castle is a beautiful example of a 'black castle' style of design. (Photo by LuxTonerre/Flickr)

of the Takeda was the immense striking power of their mounted samurai, but when the horsemen swept down upon the enemy lines, they found themselves faced by 3,000 arquebusiers. The men had been trained to fire in organised volleys and were protected by a loose palisade. The gunfire broke the impact of the initial charge and, as the second wave of horsemen prepared to go in, the gunners calmly reloaded under the protection of their spearmen. Once again the line held, and when the Takeda faltered for a third time, the samurai and footsoldiers of the Oda began to engage the attackers in hand-to-hand fighting. Several hours of conflict followed, at the end of which the Takeda withdrew after taking enormous numbers of casualties, broken forever as a military and political influence in Japan.

The brief transition between the siege of Nagashino being temporarily abandoned and the battle of Nagashino beginning, a period of time lasting but a few hours, marks an important turning point in the development of samurai warfare. The conduct of the siege itself had been no different from hundreds of other similar operations elsewhere in Japan. By contrast, the battle that followed a few hours afterwards was the herald of a military revolution. A straightforward cavalry charge, the sort that had given the Takeda their victory at Mikatagahara in 1572, was stunted by what was in effect a new type of field fortress that combined organised gunfire on a large scale with simple defence works. From this point on, Japanese warfare, in particular defensive warfare, would never be quite the same again, and when the Period of Warring States came to an end, it left behind a legacy of fortresses that provide tantalising parallels with Europe, but can be shown to be based on very different principles and with very different intentions. In castle design, as with armour and weapons, Japan once again held up a mirror to the rest of the world.

THE EVOLUTION OF THE JAPANESE CASTLE

The type of Japanese castle that Nagashino represented already had a long history. As the Japanese landscape has always had a shortage of stone and an abundance of trees clustered on mountains, it was natural that it should be the latter two factors – timber and high ground – that determined the character of Japanese fortifications for many centuries. The first Japanese castles consisted of simple wooden stockades between towers and gates that followed the natural defences provided by the height and the contours of the mountains from which the materials for the wooden walls had been taken. The erection of palisades on top of earthworks, raised by excavating a forward ditch, could compensate for the lack of high ground when a position had to be erected in an area of flatlands, but such topography was avoided wherever possible. It was from the yamashiro (mountain castles) of Akasaka and Chihaya that Kusunoki Masashige conducted his spirited defensive campaigns and guerrilla actions on behalf of Emperor Go-Daigo between 1331 and 1336.

Such designs persisted into the Sengoku Jidai. The daimyo led armies and ruled territories whose borders were defined solely by their latest conquests, and to defend their lands they adopted the yamashiro model on a huge scale. From one *honjo* (headquarters castle), a network of satellite castles radiated out, each of which had its own smaller sub-satellite, with each sub-satellite having its own local cluster of tiny guard posts. The network would often also be linked visually by a chain of fire beacons.

For a daimyo's honjo, and for most of the satellite castles, a simple stockade soon proved to be insufficient to withstand enemy attack or to provide barracks space for a large garrison, so a technique developed whereby the mountain on which the yamashiro stood was literally carved up. Using the formidable resources in manpower that successful daimyo could now command, neighbouring mountains were sculpted

ABOVE The ruins of the mountaintop Takeda Castle, built by Otagaki Mitsukage in 1441, show the commanding position of these yamashiro and the strength of the stone base. The castle was abandoned following the forced seppuku of its last lord, Akamatsu Hirohide. (Photo by Norio Nakayama/Flickr)

into a series of interlocking baileys. They followed the natural lines only in the sense that the contours provided the guide for the excavation of wide, flat, horizontal surfaces, each overlooked by the one above it.

The result was a gigantic and complex mound produced by removing materials rather than piling them up. On top of the site were placed fences, towers, stables, storehouses, walkways, bridges, gates and usually a rudimentary version of a castle keep. Very little stone was used in the construction except for strengthening the bases of gatehouses and towers and to combat soil erosion from the excavated slopes. As time went by, the simple palisades and towers inside the yamashiro were replaced by stronger wattle and daub walls, plastered over against fire attack and roofed with tiles as a protection against rain.

By the time of the battle of Nagashino it had also been realised that much larger, taller and heavier buildings could be successfully raised on top of the yamashiro if the cut-away slopes of the natural hills were reinforced with tightly packed stones. The sloping stone surfaces were designed mathematically so that any weight upon them was dissipated outwards and downwards.

This took the extra weight, and also provided a cushion against earth tremors. In addition to cutting away existing hills, similar artificial mounds were built in this way on flat areas and encased with stone. On top of the stone-clad mounds were raised primitive versions of the castle keeps that are now such an attractive feature of extant Japanese military architecture. It is unlikely that little Nagashino possessed a keep in any form other than a simple two-storey wooden building with a Japanese-style curving roof, but in one respect Nagashino Castle was exceptionally fortunate. It was not built upon a stripped-out mountain, but founded on solid rock in the form of a dramatic promontory that marked the confluence of two minor rivers that joined at Nagashino to become the mighty Toyokawa. These rocky cliffs formed two sides of an equilateral triangle, which was completed on its third side by an outer bailey of a simple ditch, mound and palisade construction.

ABOVE The site of Nagashino Castle. Very few castle remains are visible today, but the defensible situation on a rocky outcrop at the confluence of two rivers is clearly apparent in this photograph.

This combination of two impregnable rocky sides and the sheer determination of the defenders behind the wall of the third side kept every ingenious Takeda attack at bay, so Takeda Katsuyori settled down for what might have been a long wait until the defenders surrendered from starvation. But then the situation changed. A brave warrior called Torii Sune'emon slipped out of the castle and took a message to Oda Nobunaga, who immediately set out with a relieving army. But Nobunaga did not simply fall precipitately onto the rear of the Takeda lines. Instead, he halted on a low ridge a few miles away. It had a forest to its rear and left, a stream in front and a river to its right. With the aid of wooden stakes and the massed ranks of his gunners, Nobunaga converted the site into an instant castle. The battle of Nagashino was therefore won not from behind the walls of a fortress but from a simple position constructed overnight and defended by guns. Nobunaga's victory showed the effectiveness of something that had been created both temporarily and quickly.

ODA NOBUNAGA AND AZUCHI CASTLE

The graceful castle towers that we see today at places such as Himeji and Matsumoto are the most beautiful survivors from the world of the warrior and are also the legacy of Oda Nobunaga. The use of earthworks defended by massed arquebuses is one of his contributions to the development of defensive warfare. There is also another, because within a year of the battle of Nagashino this same talented general would also be demonstrating the effectiveness of the opposite extreme in castle design where huge stone walls enclosed a massive keep.

In 1576 Japan was to see the first, and perhaps the finest, of a new style of permanent military bases and palaces combined in one castle building. This was Nobunaga's castle of Azuchi, which demonstrated his power in several ways. First, its design showed the culmination of the technique of encasing the excavated hills of a yamashiro in shaped and cut stone. No bare earthen walls were now visible. All were made from graceful sloping stone and, as well as providing their own defences, these cyclopean mounds above a core of bedrock allowed the raising of a spectacular seven-storey keep ornamented within and without as befitted the grandeur to which Nobunaga aspired. Around Azuchi's central keep were a score of smaller towers, each of which would have done credit as the main keep for a normal-sized castle. Azuchi was huge, and could therefore house an enormous garrison that few daimyo could afford either to feed or to arm. Nobunaga could do both, and the internal walls of Azuchi were fitted with numerous racks for hundreds of arquebuses that could be quickly lifted down and poked out through the windows and weapon slits of the towers. The towers were also cunningly designed to enable flanking fire to be delivered from neighbouring sections.

Azuchi Castle never had to withstand a siege, and in fact its end was ignominious. Oda Nobunaga was murdered in 1582 when he was away from Azuchi on campaign and, with its master and army gone, the mighty edifice was raided and burned to the ground. But its example had served its purpose. Castle builders now knew that size mattered. In 1586 Toyotomi Hideyoshi built Osaka Castle with a large keep inside perimeter walls 12 miles in circumference. With the fall of the Hojo in 1590 Tokugawa Ieyasu acquired their fortress of Edo and set about extending it to create the mightiest castle in the land. It is now the Imperial Palace in Tokyo.

Like all the extant Japanese fortresses, Osaka no longer possesses in its entirety the original massive complex of outer works. These once stretched so far that the massive keeps we enjoy today could then have been seen from only a distance. For this reason it is difficult to assess their design from a military perspective. It is therefore

ABOVE A dramatic view of the reconstructed keep of Osaka Castle, first built by Toyotomi Hideyoshi in 1583 and modelled after Nobunaga's Azuchi Castle. (Photo by Joop/Flickr)

important to realise that the fundamental defining feature of a Japanese castle was not its ornate keep but the huge overlapping walls made from the carved stone-clad hillsides. The earliest tower keeps date only from the 1570s, and many were not added to the existing complex of smaller towers until early in the 17th century. It can also be shown from sources such as painted screens of battle exploits that the majority of the keeps that withstood attack during the time of civil wars would have been of much simpler construction than these magnificent towers. Without these encircling walls, Himeji's keep, for example, looks very vulnerable, until one realises that for an attacker to take on that graceful tower he would have had to fight through a series of formidable baileys, all of which have since disappeared. It is only when these walls are put back using one's imagination that a useful assessment may be made.

JAPANESE CASTLES IN KOREA

As noted above, we have to envisage a contemporary Japanese castle either without its tower keep or with many other encircling walls if we are to appreciate the reality of siege warfare at the end of the Period of Warring States. This is not always easy to do in Japan itself, but good examples may be found in Korea – during the invasion of 1592–98 the Japanese established a chain of coastal fortresses called *wajo* to protect their communications with Japan. As the wajo never had the tower keeps that were added later to Japanese castles, their remains provide useful information about contemporary castle design and allow a direct comparison with European models.

Instead of the Chinese and Korean 'Great Walls' snaking up and down the mountains, we see the more labour-intensive Japanese model of large-scale excavations to provide horizontal surfaces and the use of carefully designed sloping walls rather

ABOVE A view from the keep of Himeji Castle, an excellent example of the developed style, showing part of the maze of walls, gates and baileys through which the visitor must pass to access the keep. (Photo by paranoidandroid/Flickr)

than the simpler Korean walls of flat stone. Some castles had to be built very quickly, and thousands of Japanese labourers were shipped over to help with construction work, where they joined many thousands more captive Koreans. At Ulsan even the walls and gateways were incomplete as the Ming forces advanced upon it in the winter of 1597, and an eyewitness recorded the brutality meted out by the commanders to the Korean and Japanese labourers impressed to the task. Earthworks and palisades added to the hasty defences where there was no time to build with stone, and a chronicler noted how it gave the illusion that the third bailey was complete. When the Chinese attacks began, many samurai were still encamped outside the unfinished walls.

The main reason why the invaders spurned the native style of fortress design for their more permanent constructions was that nearly all the resistance put up inside Korean castles from Pusan to P'yongyang had collapsed before the initial Japanese advance, spearheaded by volleys from massed ranks of gunners. The coastal location for the wajo commanded excellent visibility out to sea and a well-defended anchorage that could in some way be linked securely to the fortress on the hill behind. The best example of this is Sunch'on, which is very well preserved. The whole area is still exactly as it was once the mountain had been scooped away and the stone facings added.

When the Chinese launched their attacks on the wajo, the theory held good and the combination of gunfire covering every angle of a simple but solid series of walls meant that the Japanese did not lose a single one of their castles. The attack on Sach'on provides an excellent illustration. There were two castles at this site: the 'old castle' was a Korean fortress taken over by the Japanese, while the 'new castle' was a wajo built on a promontory two miles to the south-west, where it overlooked the harbour and provided a safe anchorage. It was defended by Shimazu Yoshihiro and his son, Tadatsune. In preparation for their attack on Sach'on, the Chinese army advanced as far as Chinju. When four outposts were lost to the Chinese, young Shimazu Tadatsune was all for making an immediate attack, but his father forbade it. He reasoned that the Chinese army would wish to waste no time in attacking, and that the men of Satsuma were ready for them in their wajo.

This assumption proved to be correct, and the Ming army moved in for an attack at about 6.00 am on 30 October 1598 with a total of 36,700 troops. The Shimazu father and son monitored their movements from the two towers that flanked the eastern gate. Under strict orders from Yoshihiro, the Japanese held their fire, and as one or two men fell dead from Chinese arrows, Tadatsune was again for launching an attack, but once more his father urged caution.

By now the Chinese were approaching the walls, and were also attacking the main gate with a curious siege engine that combined an iron-tipped battering ram with a cannon. The joint effects of cannonball and ram smashed the gate, and soon thousands of Chinese soldiers were fighting at the entrance and climbing up the castle walls. 'Lord Yoshihiro, who saw this, gave the order to attack without delay,' writes a commentator on behalf of the Shimazu, 'and all the soldiers as one body fired their arquebuses and mowed down the enemy soldiers who were clinging on to the walls.' At this precise moment the Japanese managed to destroy the combined ram and cannon, causing its stock of gunpowder to explode with great fury right in the middle of the Ming host. A separate Shimazu chronicle implies that the engine was destroyed by a fire bomb thrown from a mortar or a catapult:

> We flung fire against the gunpowder jars, many of which had been placed within the enemy ranks. It flew from one jar to another, and the tremendous noise was carried to our ears. Consequently the alarming sound terrified all the enemy who were in the vicinity.

ABOVE The siege of Ulsan Castle during the winter of 1597/8, one of the most bitter campaigns of the Korean War.

This dramatic moment proved to be the turning point of the battle. Seeing the confusion in the Chinese ranks, Shimazu Yoshihiro led out his men in a tremendous charge. Many Chinese were cut down, but showing admirable organisation and discipline the army regrouped on a nearby hill and took the fight back to the Japanese. Some Japanese units had now become detached from the main body, and the Shimazu remained outnumbered by three to one until the approach of a relieving army from the nearest wajo at Kosong tipped the balance in Japan's favour. Thousands of Chinese were killed or pursued back as far as the Nam River, where very few stragglers managed to cross and reach the safety of Chinju. Sach'on was China's worst defeat at Japanese hands. The site is now marked by a massive burial mound containing the remains of more than 30,000 Ming troops killed by the Japanese and interred here without their noses. Those trophies were taken back to Japan as proof of duty done, and lie to this day within the erroneously named 'Ear Mound' in Kyoto.

The overall progress of the war and the death of Toyotomi Hideyoshi meant that the wajo ended up being purely defensive structures to cover the Japanese withdrawal rather than as the outposts of empire. Had things gone differently, the wajo might well have represented a parallel with the coastal forts of the Europeans, who established garrisons defended by artillery at places like Mombasa, Havana and Manila to serve as bases for overseas expansion and colonisation. Instead, the samurai returned home in defeat, and put into practice the lessons they had learned from the successful repulse of the huge assaults the Chinese had mounted on the wajo. The combination of wall and gun had held them off. In Korea the lessons learned at Nagashino and Azuchi had been subjected to their most searching test and had passed with flying colours.

ABOVE The defence of a Japanese castle using ladles of boiling water.

Within two years of their return from the Korean War the daimyo who had gone to fight abroad were to split into the two armed camps that brought about the decisive showdown at Sekigahara. A spate of castle building followed, and one daimyo in particular demonstrated in his castle the lessons that he had learned in Korea. Kato Kiyomasa had become a hero by his defence of the wajo of Ulsan, and put all that experience into his designs for Kumamoto Castle. The walls and towers were of course formidable, but he also planted nut trees inside the massive sloping stone walls to provide food during a siege. Wells were sunk, and in a curious gesture of preparation Kato Kiyomasa ordered that the tatami floor mats inside the towers should be stuffed not with rice straw but with vegetable stalks so that a desperate garrison could literally eat the floor.

Castles similar to Kumamoto were to be found in every province until, with the achievement of Tokugawa supremacy, the daimyo were ordered to demolish every castle in their territories except one. The resulting edifices, many of which still exist today, brought the evolution from sculpted mountain to military palace to a level of perfection in terms of architecture and military necessity. The development in castle design from mountain stockade to fortress of stone was therefore complete.

THE LAST SAMURAI

To some extent the consequences of the wars of the Sengoku Jidai may be felt in Japan to this day, not as a direct result of the fighting that took place so long ago, but more because of the isolationist measures the Tokugawa shoguns then put in place to prevent any more wars. One major element was the *baku-han* system, whereby national government was provided by the bakufu (shogunate), and local government by the han (daimyo's fiefs).

Like everything else in Tokugawa Japan, there were regulations governing the smallest detail of everyday life. The daimyo's castle became the focal point for local administration, and many were rebuilt or extended. Yet along with the rebuilding and redevelopment of provincial castles, many were destroyed under the policy of 'one province, one castle'. The result was that the mighty fortresses we see today became the centre of a daimyo's territory in a more decisive and defined way than ever before. Some, such as Himeji, Matsumoto and Hikone, are perfectly preserved. Trade flourished in the castle towns, and many merchants grew richer than the samurai, who were supposed to have no trade beyond that of serving as a loyal warrior.

LEFT Some of the first photographs of samurai were taken by Felice Beato. In this hand-coloured 1867 portrait, a Japanese soldier sits next to a tall bow and a bundle of arrows. (Photo by Felice Beato/ Hulton Archive/Getty Images)

ABOVE Ship of Commodore Matthew C. Perry's American expedition to Japan of 1852–54. Perry sailed into Tokyo's Uraga Harbour with a squadron of four steam frigates. The Japanese agreed to open diplomatic and trade links with the USA, but the American 'black ships' came to be seen, and resented by many Japanese, as symbols of threatening Western technology and colonialism. (Photo by Ann Ronan Pictures/Print Collector/Getty Images)

The additional policy of settling potential rebels in distant fiefs with loyal daimyo to watch over them was enhanced by a development of the Japanese tradition of taking hostages to ensure good behaviour. So while all the daimyo lived in their castle towns from where they governed their provinces, their wives and children were required to live in Edo, right under the eyes of the shogun. The wisdom of this move was seen in 1638 when the Shimabara Rebellion broke out. It started as a peasant revolt and drew in dispossessed samurai; none of the daimyo broke ranks to join them. The final refinement of the system was to require the daimyo to make regular visits to Edo to pay their respects to the shogun. This had the result of forcing all the armies of Japan to spend most of their time and resources marching from one end of the archipelago to the other.

The next measure was a complete reversal of the policy of encouraging foreign trade and exploration that had characterised the first decade of the 17th century and led to such adventurers as Yamada Nagamasa sailing to Formosa (Taiwan) and Siam (Thailand). Instead Tokugawa Japan increasingly turned in on itself. Fear of European influence led first to a ban on Christianity and then to a ban on foreign trade. Only China and Korea were exempt, and their trade contacts were strictly controlled. Apart from a tiny trading post called Dejima in Nagasaki harbour, where the Protestant Dutch (who could be relied upon not to spread the Jesuits' messages) were allowed very limited access, Japan closed its doors to the outside world. All these measures came about because the Tokugawa shoguns feared a return to the dark days of the Sengoku Jidai. Two centuries of peace followed, out of which emerged modern Japan and a world very different from the one that had once known a century and a half of war.

Japan's isolation came to an end in July 1853 when four American warships entered the harbour of Uraga, at the entrance to Edo Bay. They were commanded by

Commodore Matthew C. Perry, who bore a letter from President Millard Fillmore demanding that Japan sign a treaty of friendship with the United States. It was a defining moment in Japanese history. Fifteen years later the shogunate was abolished, the emperor was restored and Japan entered the modern world.

The enterprise is known to history as the Meiji Restoration, and presents a popular image of ex-samurai in top hats standing with their wives in crinolines to watch steam trains go by. But although it is customarily portrayed as a peaceful transition, the events that surrounded the Meiji Restoration saw conflicts as bitter as any that had erupted during the Period of Warring States.

In 1860, Ii Naosuke, head of a family loyal to the Tokugawa shogun, was torn from his palanquin in Edo (Tokyo) and hacked to death by a group of anti-shogun and anti-Western terrorists who wanted to abolish the shogunate. He had been closely involved in the negotiations between the shogunate and the diplomats of countries such as the United States, who sought to establish trading links with Japan from 1854 onwards. In this the shogunate had proved to be considerably far-sighted, but this was not to the liking of their rivals, who wanted to expel all the 'barbarians', as they called the Western interlopers. Ii Naosuke persisted in his belief that Japan should open its doors to the outside world.

In the year after Ii Naosuke's death the shogun's government trod carefully. Its members were sensitive to criticism, suspicious of the foreigner and fully aware of the threat posed by fanatical loyalists who wanted nothing more than the shogun's disappearance from the scene. There were so many matters to decide. Should the country be opened up or not? Were the existing treaties fair to Japan? And could the foreign powers ever be resisted, given their evident military superiority?

FANATICS FROM CHOSHU

The slogan of the loyalists was 'Sonno Joi' ('Honour the emperor and expel the barbarians'), and with the extremist faction now so dominant in Kyoto, pressure was put on the shogun to set a definite date for the expulsion of the foreigners. The representatives from Choshu, the domain of the Mori family, were particularly insistent upon this point, and sent a letter to the court asking for a date to be fixed so that Choshu could prepare for action. If the shogun would not expel the foreigners, then the emperor himself should lead his troops. Further vacillation by the shogun prompted a new round of terror.

The attitude being shown by Choshu, who held the dominant position in Kyoto, greatly alarmed other han. Many shared their views, but feared that Choshu's belligerence would lead to disaster. Matsudaira Katamori of Aizu was a key figure in these deliberations, and in the autumn of 1863 joined the other influential han of Satsuma in carrying out a coup against Choshu.

Choshu's influence at court was greatly curtailed following this incident, but back in Choshu itself matters grew steadily worse. Foreign ships were fired on as they passed through the Shimonoseki Straits, provoking a massive counter-bombardment from a joint fleet comprising ships from Great Britain, France, the Netherlands and the United States. Within a day the Choshu forts had been demolished and their troops defeated by foreign landing parties. It seemed to the shogun that the time had come to march against Choshu and by the end of 1864, 150,000 samurai were poised at its borders, ready to attack. Matsudaira Katamori was originally chosen to lead the expedition, but it was felt that his role in Kyoto was too important to be even temporarily abandoned. The expedition was no less successful for that, and returned from Choshu with the severed heads of Choshu's leaders.

THE MEIJI RESTORATION

If the bakufu thought they had solved the problem of Choshu, they were wrong, because a civil war within the han gave Choshu new leaders who were even more radical than the ones who had formerly led the rebellion. Satsuma, too, felt aggrieved that it had not been given a voice in politics commensurate with its supportive role in 1863. Satsuma therefore withdrew from the Kyoto coalition and entered into a secret pact with Choshu. The restoration of the emperor was at last possible, so in January 1868 an alliance of Satsuma, Choshu and other han seized the Kyoto palace and proclaimed the return of imperial rule. As its first act, the new Meiji government stripped the shogun of his lands and abolished all bakufu offices.

Despite the withdrawal of the shogun Tokugawa Yoshinobu to a temple to await news of his fate, a sizeable core of pro-Tokugawa support still existed in northern Japan, primarily in the province of Aizu, the han of Matsudaira Katamori. The subsequent campaign to crush these dissenters culminated in the dramatic events of the siege of Aizu-Wakamatsu Castle and the tragic fate of the White Tigers, a group of 16- and 17-year-old youths who had escaped a brush with much greater numbers of government troops but mistakenly took smoke arising from a fire at the castle to mean that the keep had fallen. In classic samurai style, they prepared themselves for death – some writing poems, some acting as seconds for their friends – and all committed seppuku within sight of the castle. The castle defenders, men and women of all ages and social classes, mounted a brave defence, but after a month of enduring the siege Aizu-Wakamatsu finally fell.

In a cruel act of retribution, the Meiji rulers confiscated the entire han of Aizu, and the following year sent the surviving samurai to detention camps. Their later exile to the remote and inhospitable peninsula in Aomori was a sad end to such

a late flowering of samurai heroism.

The reforms continued and over the following years the tax reforms and land seizures continued the effective abolition of the samurai class. In 1873 the new government instituted conscription, requiring four years' military service and three years in the reserve from every male on reaching 21. This represented a fundamental change to the status of the samurai, who had enjoyed the privilege of being the only class permitted to carry weapons. In addition, samurai were no longer allowed to carry the swords that were the badge of this status.

The reforms of the Meiji Restoration flew in the face of the founding fathers' tradition and isolationism, who had opposed the Tokugawa shogunate's engagement with foreign influence. The abolition of the samurai class was the most severe blow of all, and it is not surprising that the events of 1876 provoked a reaction

ABOVE Portrait of the Meiji Emperor, in about 1904. (Library of Congress, Washington)

from fanatics among the ranks of former samurai. Several insurrections and outrages occurred elsewhere in Japan during that momentous year, but all were put down quickly and efficiently by Japan's new conscript army.

THE SATSUMA REBELLION

Then, early in 1877, a further rising happened. It was a samurai revolt on a scale much larger and more serious than any that had preceded it. It was led by Japan's most famous general, and it originated from Japan's most formidable samurai clan. It is known in Japanese history as the *Seinan Senso*, a title which simply means 'the war in the south-west'. To western historians it is remembered as the Satsuma Rebellion.

To understand the origins of the Satsuma Rebellion it is necessary to backtrack somewhat to describe what had happened to Satsuma in the years following the Meiji Restoration. Frustrated by the Western-style reformers, Saigo Takamori, one of the great leaders of the Meiji Restoration, had withdrawn from the government in October 1873 and retired to his native Satsuma. There he had set up 120 'Private Schools', effectively military academies to train a Satsuma-led private army. Candidates were required to swear an oath that they would be faithful unto death, and then to seal it with their own blood. Not surprisingly, the Meiji government in Tokyo became alarmed by these developments. Also, as the Satsuma clan had been instrumental in establishing the Meiji regime in the first place, a large quantity of imperial arms and ammunition was located in Kagoshima. With the growth of the Private Schools, the Tokyo authorities decided to transfer the entire contents of the Kagoshima arsenal to Osaka, and in a secret night operation on 30 January 1877 a ship was sent to collect the equipment. Their arrival was discovered, and the ship's crew found themselves

attacked by more than 1,000 Satsuma warriors. The government officials fled empty-handed, and the Satsuma samurai seized the imperial arsenal for their own.

On 13 February 1877, the Satsuma soldiers from the Private Schools were organised into tactical units. In essence, Satsuma now had its own army. A European correspondent wrote:

ABOVE The 20 White Tigers, of whom 11 were 17 years old and nine were only 16, commit hara kiri. They had sufficient time to perform the act in classic samurai style, their grandstand view of the collapse of Aizu's hopes adding further drama to the scene.

ABOVE The keep of Aizu-Wakamatsu Castle viewed under snow. In 1868 this became the site of one of the last and most violent battles to be conducted against a Japanese castle.

Saigo's men were but partly armed with rifles. Most of them were equipped with the keen double-handed swords of feudal times and with daggers and spears. It seemed to be their opinion that patrician samurai could rush into close quarters with the *heimin* (common people) and easily rout them – granting even that they were armed with rifles and bayonets. And it was reported that the astute Saigo ordered his soldiers not to kill the poor plebs in the government ranks, but rather to slash them well about the legs so as to disable them and render it necessary for each man thus wounded to be borne off the field by two able-bodied comrades – thus depriving the opposing ranks of three soldiers instead of one.

This passage is undoubtedly a romantic exaggeration. Saigo Takamori was not such an extreme conservative as to believe that samurai swords and bravery were all that a modern army needed. The sword was indeed the universal weapon, but in addition they carried Snider and Enfield rifles, some carbines and pistols, and enough ammunition for about 100 rounds per man. The training in the Private Schools had also included artillery and engineering techniques from the West.

SAIGO TAKAMORI GOES TO WAR

On 15 February 1877, under deep snow, Saigo's advance guard left Kagoshima for the north. Romantic spirits among the samurai saw symbolic significance in the snow, for it had been on a snowy night that the famous 47 Ronin had carried out their celebrated deed of vengeance. There was also a poignant echo from Japanese history as Saigo Takamori bade farewell to his 12-year-old son in the way of the hero Kusunoki Masashige. With such analogies ringing in their ears, the Satsuma army headed for their first objective: Kumamoto Castle.

Kumamoto was the castle into which Kato Kiyomasa had poured all the experience he had gained during the Korean War. When the Meiji government had taken over responsibility for the army from the individual daimyo, they had established area commands throughout Japan. The command for Kyushu was based at Kumamoto, confirming the importance that Kato Kiyomasa had originally envisaged for it. The castle was also the only major obstacle in the way of Saigo Takamori marching his men through Kyushu and on eventually to Tokyo. Beyond Kumamoto was the road to the strategic port of Nagasaki, which would provide Saigo with sea transport and help him secure a hold over the whole of Kyushu.

Saigo Takamori expected either that the Kumamoto garrison would let him pass unhindered, or that overcoming it would be an easy matter. He knew that in the garrison were many survivors of a bizarre suicide raid by fanatical samurai the year before. The group had called themselves 'the League of the Divine Wind', in other words kamikaze, and carried out a raid in which they killed 300 of the imperial garrison with their samurai swords, then fled to the hills where some committed seppuku and others surrendered or were killed by the pursuing troops.

With this recent precedent in mind the vanguard of the Satsuma army reached Kawashiri, a short distance south of Kumamoto, on 19 February and, finding the road blocked by imperial troops, established a headquarters base. Meanwhile the Tokyo government had not been idle. Ships were steaming towards Hakata and Nagasaki with reinforcements. The first shots of the Satsuma Rebellion were fired at 1.15 pm on 21 February when the troops of the Kumamoto garrison who had blocked Saigo's advance at Kawashiri opened fire on the rebels. The imperial troops were quickly overcome and withdrew into the shelter of Kumamoto. Outside its walls now sat Saigo Takamori with a Satsuma army that was three times larger than the imperial garrison. One of Saigo's subordinates, who had once himself been in command at Kumamoto, advocated an all-out assault. Saigo's decision was for a more planned approach, with a frontal attack from the south-east by 2,500 troops and a rear attack by 3,000 from the north-west, holding back 3,400 men in reserve. All other troops were occupied with reconnoitring the movements of any other imperial troops that might have been approaching.

THE SIEGE OF KUMAMOTO

Leading the garrison of Kumamoto was General Tani Tateki. In the romantic legends that surround the image of Saigo Takamori as 'the last of the samurai' there is little space for a regular, Westernised soldier. But brave Tani deserves more recognition that he customarily receives. Under his command was a garrison of about 3,800 men. General Tani knew that the fate of Japan depended on him holding Kumamoto against Saigo until the full imperial army could throw its strength against him.

Tani lacked information about his enemy, and the humiliating tragedy of the suicide attack the previous year had left the garrison badly shaken. Moreover, many of Tani's officers were themselves natives of Satsuma and he could not be sure how the townspeople would react to finding themselves in the midst of civil war.

This is not to say that General Tani was unprepared. From the time that the first reports had reached him of Saigo's intentions, he had secretly augmented the castle's defences with ammunition dumps, bamboo fences and landmines. At the same time, he made a grand show of carrying out memorial services for the men killed during the suicide attack, hoping thereby to identify the interests of the local people with that of the imperial garrison.

Tani suffered a setback when fire broke out in a large storehouse on 19 February, destroying nearly all of the castle's food supply. Worse, the fire quickly spread and soon threatened the castle's ammunition reserve. Fortunately, the storehouse collapsed, falling inwards and away from the explosives. Not only was the precious ammunition saved, but the shared danger forged a bond between officers and men that had not previously existed, and the defenders of Kumamoto began to gel as one. Over the next few days a furious attempt was made to buy up all the available food from Kumamoto city, and on 20 February a welcome reinforcement of 600 police troops arrived. Now confident of local support, Tani reluctantly ordered the destruction of several hundred local houses to provide a clear field of fire. The sluices were opened to let the moats fill with water, and Kumamoto waited, ready for the rebel assault, like 'fish in a kettle'.

ABOVE Saigo Takamori is shown here in a hanging scroll that illustrates the size of the man, who was large in personality as well as physique.

Saigo's first move against Kumamoto was heralded by the rather quaint action of firing 'arrow letters' into the castle calling upon the defenders to surrender. The text included the following words: 'As we feel pity for those who have been compelled to remain in the castle against their will, we will pardon them if they at once throw down their arms and submit to us.' The exhortations produced no response, and in the early hours of 22 February the advance guard of the Satsuma army began their assault on Kumamoto Castle from the south-east. As the hours went by, the attack spread round the outer walls and small-arms fire could be heard coming from all directions. For the next two days, furious attacks were carried out on the castle ramparts. The Satsuma samurai, their ancestral swords in hand, clambered up the walls like suicide squads to be shot down by the rifle fire from Tani's conscript army. Tani's men held firm, and no foothold was gained by 24 February, at which point Saigo regrouped and withdrew 2,000 out of his original attacking force of 5,000 to move north to await the imperial reinforcements that he knew would be on their way.

The siege then developed into a war of attrition, with casualties mounting on both sides of Kumamoto's walls. Saigo now managed, against all the odds, to fight on three fronts: against the castle, against the imperialists in the south and soon against a huge reinforcement that moved down from the north. He began a bombardment from artillery positions on the hills around the castle, and frustrated attempts by the garrison to contact the outside world. Eventually Shishido Masateru, a former superintendent of the castle, managed to slip through the siege lines disguised as a carpenter and contact the imperial army. His safe return with the news that relief was on its way greatly encouraged everyone within. General Tani and Shishido are the only two people ever to have had their lives commemorated with a statue inside Kumamoto Castle.

By 1 March the castle had probably only 19 days of rations left, and ammunition was so limited that the defenders had begun digging up unexploded Satsuma shells and firing them back at the besiegers. As the siege progressed, the Satsuma lines moved ever nearer to the castle walls, and at one point got so close that the opponents were able to exchange banter with one another. As is so often the case in a civil war, fathers encountered sons, and brother met with brother fighting on the other side.

The supply of fresh vegetables was soon exhausted; meals of rice and barley were restricted to two per day for combatants, while non-combatants received only gruel. The interior moats were drained to a minimum to make it easier to catch the fish within them, in spite of the obvious advantage it gave to the enemy. The killing of a horse was a cause for rejoicing as the dead animal was immediately cooked and eaten. The rationing helped the garrison eke out their food supply longer than expected.

On 7 April Major Oku Yasukata led a detachment out of the castle to link up with the imperial troops known to be in the south near Kawashiri. The operation was a success, and Oku managed to seize some supplies and held the road to Kumamoto open long enough for the garrison to be enriched by the addition of 100 rifles, 3,000 rounds of ammunition and several hundred bags of rice. When the Satsuma army finally cut the road, Oku broke through again and joined up with the imperialists in Kawashiri.

By mid-April, the pressure from the imperial army was beginning to tell, but Saigo's excellent generalship prevented them from relieving the castle. Meanwhile the advance from the south continued like the sweep from the hand of a clock. The orders were to stand firm as soon as they had secured positions on the north bank of the Midori River. Kumamoto might not have been relieved for some time had it not been for a certain Lieutenant-Colonel Yamakawa, whose subsequent conduct reminded the rest of the imperial army that the spirit of the samurai was not quite

dead among the imperial troops. Instead of halting, he continued his advance, and at about 4.00 pm he appeared in front of the castle gate to relieve the castle on his own.

An imperial soldier stood at the gates of Kumamoto. All firing had ceased, and pausing for a moment to identify the new arrivals, those in the garrison soon realised that the ordeal was now over.

ABOVE A print by Yoshitoshi showing the battle around Kumamoto. (www.lacma.org)

A SYMBOLIC END

The relief of Kumamoto Castle was the turning point in the Satsuma Rebellion. Between April and September 1877, the course of the action dwindled to a series of pursuits and dispersals across southern Kyushu. Once the siege of Kumamoto had ended, the government troops concentrated their efforts on taking Kagoshima, where Saigo had fled with a now pitifully small number of followers.

Together with only a few hundred men Saigo took up a position on Shiroyama, the site of the former castle of the mighty Shimazu at the centre of the city. Thirty thousand government troops slowly closed in on him. By all accounts Saigo Takamori had already made up his mind either to be killed in battle or to die by his own hand. The night before the final assault he behaved like the samurai of old, listening to the music of the Satsuma lute, performing an ancient sword dance, and composing poetry:

> If I were a drop of dew
> I could take shelter on a leaftip
> But, being a man
> I have no place in this whole world.

He then exchanged cups of sake with his chief officers, and prepared for the attack by the government forces that began at 4.00 the following morning. Saigo and his followers moved down the hill under intense enemy fire. Soon he was hit in the groin by a bullet and could no longer walk. His follower Beppu Shinsuke lifted him up and carried him down the mountain until they came to a place that Saigo regarded as suitable for seppuku. It was the gate of a former mansion of the Shimazu. Saigo

ABOVE This impressive view of the reconstructed keep of Kumamoto Castle shows the imposing height of the stone walls. The overhang of the superstructure allowed for dropping of rocks to clear the walls. (Photo by Thilo Hilbere/Flickr)

bowed in the direction of the imperial palace and then cut himself open. Beppu Shinusuke acted as his second, and as soon as Saigo's head was safely disposed of he charged down the hill and was mown down by gunfire.

The Satsuma Rebellion was the last organised attempt until the 1930s to oppose the government by force. Japan's last samurai army had been pitted against a force of conscripted farmers, and had failed. More than 60,000 imperial troops fought in the Satsuma Rebellion and suffered 7,000 deaths and 9,000 wounded. Of the total rebel strength of 30,000 only a handful survived. The symbolic effect of the defeat was every bit as dramatic. The Western correspondent quoted above had watched the imperial force leave Tokyo, and had written:

> Someone said that the heimin, or common people, comprising a large part of the imperial forces, would never be able to face the samurai of Satsuma – that one samurai would put five heimin to flight, and as the troops marched through Tokyo on their way south they were the recipients of pitying comments that they were but so much meat for Saigo's swords.

That such comments were proved wrong was the death blow for the samurai class. The belief that only samurai could fight had been finally and dramatically laid to rest around the walls of Kumamoto Castle, and the death of Saigo Takamori at Shiroyama was but the confirmation of it. As for Kumamoto Castle, although much of it was destroyed in the fighting, the ghost of Kato Kiyomasa could have looked down upon the scene with much satisfaction. Modern artillery, possessing a power

LEFT The Uto tower, one of the surviving original elements of Kumamoto Castle. Here the daunting height of the stone wall and the opening for dropping of rocks can be seen.

he could only have dreamed of, had failed to shatter the huge stone foundations on which it lay. His wells had ensured that the garrison never suffered from thirst, and his walls proved a fine defence against the swinging sword blades with which Kiyomasa would have been so familiar. Kato Kiyomasa's dream of an impregnable castle had been tested and proved against an enemy that he would have recognised and understood. They may have carried rifles in addition to their swords and used modern cannon, but Kumamoto had withstood the final siege of a Japanese castle by an army that was predominantly driven by the ideals and technology of the world of the samurai.

GLOSSARY

ashigaru	footsoldiers
baku-han	system whereby national government was provided by the bakufu, and local government by the han
bakufu	the shogun's government
bokken	a practice sword
bushi	samurai, warrior
bushido	the way of the warrior
daimyo	'great name' – the head of a great samurai family
daisho	the pair of swords, katana and wakizashi, which was the exclusive privilege of the samurai
do	body armour
do-maru	form of armour
emishi	aboriginal tribesmen of northern Japan
genpuku (genbuku)	coming of age
hachimaki	headband
haidate	thigh armour
hakama	wide trousers
han	a daimyo's fief

ABOVE Great determination is shown on the face of this samurai as he engages a rival in single combat. His helmet is ornamented with deer antlers.

haori	loose jacket
hara kiri	'belly-cutting': an alternate way of describing seppuku
haramaki-do	form or armour
hayago	matchlock cartridges
heimin	common people
honjin	main camp, the command centre of an army in the field
honjo	a daimyo's main castle
horo	a type of sashimono in the form of a cloak stretched over a bamboo frame
ikki	associations created by low-ranking samurai families for mutual protection
Ikko-ikki	'Single-minded League': associations who rose against daimyo rule in the 15th and 16th centuries
jinja	Shinto shrine
junshi	suicide by followers or family after another's death
kabuto	helmet
kaishaku	a second who performs the act of cutting off the head in the process of seppuku
kakun	rules set by the daimyo for their clans
kami	spirits or deities central to Japan's Shinto religion
kamikaze	the 'wind of the gods'
kanshi	suicide as a protest
kata	a series of set moves in martial arts
kataki uchi	the Tokugawa system of registered vendetta
katana	the samurai sword

kendo	'the way of the sword'
kenjutsu	sword techniques
kimono	garment resembling a robe that wraps around the body
koku	a unit of rice able to feed a man for a year (120 litres)
kote	sleeve armour
kozane	small scales used in armour
kyuba no michi	the way of horse and bow
maku	the curtains that surround a general's headquarters on a battlefield
menpo	face mask
mon	family crest
monto	followers of the Buddhist sect of Jodo Shinshu
naginata	a long-bladed polearm
nodachi	extremely long sword with a long handle
nodowa	throat protector
o-yoroi	form of samurai body armour
obi	waist sash
okegawa-do	late form of armour
ronin	masterless samurai
sake	rice wine
same	'sharkskin' – usually the skin of a giant ray, used for the katana's grip
sashimono	an identifying device carried by samurai to show allegiance
saya	sword scabbard
Sengoku Jidai	the Period of Warring States
sensei	teacher or master

seppuku	ritual suicide by cutting open the abdomen; also called hara kiri
shikken	regency
shikoro	neck guard
shogun	military dictator
sode	shoulder plate armour
sokotsu-shi	expiatory suicide
suneate	shin armour
tachi-do	standing cuirass
tanto	dagger
tatami	rice-straw mat
tokonoma	alcove to display a hanging scroll or flower arrangement
torii	the distinctive gateway of a Shinto shrine
tosei gusoku	modern armour
tsuba	sword guard
tsumeru	the practice technique of pulling one's blows
uji	ancient clans
utsubo	quiver
wajo	Japanese-style fortresses built during the invasion of Korea
wakizashi	a short sword, often worn paired with the katana
yabusame	the sport of horse archery
yamashiro	castle built on a mountain top
yari	spear
yarijutsu	spear techniques
yashiki	mansion
yumi	the samurai bow